A GRAIN OF TRUTH

Descended from the same North-East family as Robert Burns, Jack Webster was born and brought up in Aberdeenshire. He started his newspaper career in Turiff before moving on to Aberdeen Journals and later the Express empire of Lord Beaverbrook. He then joined the *Sunday Standard*, and is now a columnist on the *Glasgow Herald*.

Jack Webster's books include *The Dons*, a history of Aberdeen Football Club, and *Gordon Strachan*, the biography of the Aberdeen, Manchester United and Scotland football star. His first attempt at writing for television was the 1986 award-winning film which took the title of this book, *A Grain of Truth*, and told the story of the final day at his father's farm at Maud.

Jack Webster is married and has three sons, all in journalism.

JACK WEBSTER

A Grain of Truth

A Scottish Journalist Remembers

Fontana/Collins

First published by Paul Harris Publishing, Edinburgh, 1981
First issued in Fontana Paperbacks 1987

Copyright © Jack Webster 1981

Made and printed in Great Britain by
William Collins Sons & Co. Ltd, Glasgow

For my sons
Geoffrey, Keith and Martin
who inherit the tradition
– and remembering
my beloved younger cousins
Greig Watt and Arthur Argo
who lives were cut tragically short

CONTENTS

ACKNOWLEDGEMENTS

My thanks for photographic assistance to: Photo Service of Peterhead, David Sutherland and library staff of Aberdeen Journals, George M. Wilson, formerly of Fraserburgh, the *Scottish Daily Express*, and to Ron Stenberg for his sketch.

Chapter One

Come into the Garden

In the searing heat of 1947, that most glorious of twentieth century summers, they carried my bed to the front green of our council house in the village of Maud, Aberdeenshire, in the hope that it would hasten recuperation from a serious heart condition. I was just a boy in the sixteenth summer of life and there, under the cool of a garden shelter, I lay pale and limp, still smarting from the long series of cardiographs and blood tests, the shaking of heads and vague talk of leaking valves and murmurs which seemed like a fair concoction of doom. How psychologically damaging to discover that your life has apparently been defused before it has properly started; on top of which I was burdened with a painful stammer.

So there I lay as douce village folk came past and stopped for a cheery word; and when they had gone I would listen to that strange harmony of summer sounds which can swell a silence into an oratorio, and then I would drift into the day-dream of a future that I had long envisaged. That future had now been cancelled, or so they said, as Professor Craig of Aberdeen looked down with kindly understanding and pronounced that I was 'a very tired boy'. If I were to work at all it would have to be behind an office desk.

That boyhood dream of being a journalist, which had lived with me for as long as I could remember, was now an option to put firmly out of my mind in favour of a job in an office. I gulped hard and felt an added weight descending upon an already over-burdened heart. But when the tears had been wiped away and a loving mother had given a glimmer of encour-

1

agement, there emerged a new resolution: If life ran the risk of being so limited then it had better be spent in the things I enjoyed. 'No journalism' did they say? Ever so slowly a smile broke over a tear-stained face and I could swear that from that moment onwards, the good Lord put a healing hand on a faulty heart. . . .

The memory of it all was with me still, more than thirty years later, as I drove north towards Aberdeen on a journey which was filled with poignant expectation. For there I was, driving forward into the past on a mission of re-discovery, seeking to stand once more on the plains of North-East Scotland, at the place where I began, to take stock of the journey so far.

Since that summer of 1947 every day had been a bonus as skeely nature patched those cardiac cracks and enabled me to plod my way through the cherished dream of journalism via the varied empires of Lord Kemsley, Lord Beaverbrook and Willie Peters of Turriff.

That dicky heart had been put to the test in the chair of Chief Sub-editor of the *Scottish Sunday Express* and more strenuously in the varied wanderings of a writing newspaperman. As a features writer with the *Scottish Daily Express* I had dodged the bombs and bullets of Belfast, strolled among the Chinese hovels of Hong Kong and Singapore, slept rough in the jungles of Malaysia, walked rather appropriately with the afflicted to the shrine of Lourdes – and done some pretty banal and boring things as well. The pursuit of a life with a modest expectation had taken me across the Atlantic on the old *Queen Mary*, inside the White House of Washington and the Kremlin of Moscow, as well as face to face with a buffalo as I rode across the Badlands of the American Mid-West.

Fascinating hours in the company of people like Charlie Chaplin, Bing Crosby, Paul Getty, Mohammed Ali and Montgomery of Alamein (not to mention Shirley Bassey, Bill Haley and a few Prime Ministers!) may have seemed light years away from my thoughts as I sat back at the wheel of the motor car and sought to absorb every nook and nuance of landscape and emotion as they washed towards me.

Somehow the time had come to fit them all into the over-all pattern of one man's life, however ill-matched some parts of that jigsaw may have seemed. Only then, having drawn all the threads together, could you step back and view the whole tapestry in perspective, giving yourself a therapy to clear the mind and fortify the soul. That was my mission on this northward journey which was already filling me with a mixture of excitement and a sense of well-being.

As the blue hills of Perthshire and the distant Cairngorms faded suitably away to the left I found myself pondering a popular misconception that 'north' is Highland and 'south' is Lowland, whereas the division is much more east and west. For that very reason, Glasgow is arguably a Highland city and Aberdeen is a thoroughly Lowland one, the Aberdonians having driven out the Highlanders at the Battle of Harlaw and maintained a pretty cool welcome ever since.

So the high lands were taking their white caps and peaks into the mists and mysteries of a spacious west and leaving me to continue my journey over mild undulations by Forfar and Brechin towards that most distinctive of Scottish corners, the North-East.

Through Laurencekirk to the red soil of the Mearns and a fresh excitement stirred my veins at the first whiff of the North-East atmosphere and the knowledge that the land of my begetting was racing towards me, mile by mile, minute by minute. Did she come with arms outstretched to enfold a returning son or with the rolling-pin of chastisement to scold a deserter?

That majestic sweep of land between the foothills of the Grampians and the Kincardineshire coast stirred nostalgic thoughts of my literary hero, Lewis Grassic Gibbon, the loon from Arbuthnott who made this land speak with a voice that was deep and warm and abiding.

That brought me to the lip of the gorge by which I must follow the path of a snake into the pit of Stonehaven, with its neat harbour and town square and sharply-rising mansions to the left. Now the road marched high by Portlethen and with the sudden flair of a magician unfolded the cloak of Aberdeen, that

sparkling gem of British cities. There it lay in all its granite
glory, sloping majestically towards the North Sea as the winter
sun drew a dance of light from the rare reflection of the Rubis-
law masonry.

An acceleration of pride was burning in my Buchan breast as
I surveyed it on the downward drive towards the Brig o' Dee.
Soon you lose the elevation and glide along the banks of the
river by the football pitches, proud in a sudden awareness that
this Granite City and its couthy hinterland are now well known
around the world as more than just a hackneyed joke about
meanness. For that of course we had to thank oil, which had
put into the pronunciation of Aberdeen an international ring to
compare with Houston.

As I drove up Holburn Street and down the grace of Union
Street, I was struck by the humorous thought that my shrewd
and canny kinsmen were sitting on a veritable fortune all that
time (seventy-five million years at a rough guess) and didn't
know it! How rough is the justice of the cruel, cruel sea, I was
telling myself, as I passed C & A's at the top of Bridge Street
and remembered that there had stood the queen of all Aberdeen
hotels, the Palace, before it was burned down in 1941.

Imagine the effrontery of it that total strangers from alien
cultures had managed to scoop up the prize of oil from under
the noses of hard-headed people in whose company, it used to
be said, the business-like Jews found it so difficult to survive
that most of them fled the city a long time ago.

Then I had to drive on down King Street, across the Bridge
of Don and out along the dual carriageway – or the double road,
as we always called it – for my real destination was yet to come.
They had improved the road to Ellon, long since cutting out
that suicidal bend at Tipperty where incautious drivers were
liable to make an involuntary call at the wee shoppie on the
corner, across from the brickworks. So to Ellon, now a sprawl
of oilmen's dormitories they said, and straight ahead at the
roundabout where the Buchan boundary more or less begins.

The route past Arnage estate reminded me there was once a
little boy called Donald Stewart who grew up in a cottage in one

of the fields. He looked towards the imposing Arnage Castle and vowed to his widowed mother that one day he would own the place. Donald was as good as his word. By his early thirties he was a wealthy builder at the Bridge of Don and when he finally acquired the spacious residence he invited my parents and me to expensive parties where the adults drank and danced, children played games and we all gathered round to hear a virtuoso performance by a shy and elderly gentleman whose name was John Storrie. The particular fascination was that he laid across his knee an instrument which he then plugged into an electric socket before widening our eyes in wonder and twanging us from the cold Howe of Arnage to the heat of Hawaii with a sound I had never heard before. That was our introduction to the electric guitar, most of a generation before it became a weapon of assault upon the tenderness of the human eardrum.

But Auchnagatt awaited, not much of a place in size, but once boasting a flock of local farmers whose consumption at the Baron's Hotel would have drowned all other claims to alcoholic capacity. Past Nethermuir House, I turned right at the road-sign which said 'MAUD 2' and embarked on that final drive, along by places like Drymuir and Pitfoskie, where my uncle Jimmy still farmed. It was the most poignant stage of all as the road rose gently then suddenly presented you with the village of Maud below. There it was, spread out for all to see in the hollow valley, well off the beaten track of the tourist yet at the very heart of the area known as Buchan, famed for its beef cattle and broad humour and the barley which had ousted the great industry of oats.

You might well pass through it, unmoved, or miss it altoge-ther if I did not pull you up by my side and let you into the secret of what it means to the eye of this particular beholder. For this Maud which gave me birth and a wealth of childhood memories may well be the last place on God's earth, as some uncharitable people have said; to which I can only reply that the good Lord kept the best until last.

I descended that last half mile into the village at the slow pace of reverence so that no part of the arrival would escape my senses. It was all so familiar that I might never have been away – Fedderate Cottages where I was born, the School, the old Poorhouse, the railway station now derelict; and the front green of 2 Park Crescent where I had lain ill that scorching summer. This was it. I was home in the place where I belonged, home in my own dour, rugged North-East corner of Scotland which has more romance in its story than many a distant place with colourful reputation.

As I gazed around and spotted the farm of Honeyneuk, I was reminded of an incident involving an eccentric acquaintance of my childhood, Willie Paul, who farmed there. Willie was a strange mixture of good heart and bad temper who would flare into a fearsome rage on occasion, with his bonnet stuck on at an angle to his nose. When a persistent taxman came round one day to make some tactful inquiry about a balance which was due to His Majesty's Inspector of Taxes, the doughty Willie got out his cartridges, pulled the double-barrelled gun from the hallstand and advanced upon the bowler-hatted bureaucrat as he came up the farm close, shouting 'Get oot o' here, ye bugger o' hell, or I'll sheet ye!' The inoffensive member of His Majesty's Inspectorate was last seen disappearing in the general direction of Maud, perhaps not fully aware of how narrowly he had escaped the discomfort of a shower of gunshot in his backside. Willie claimed that he had shot better rabbits than that.

When he died, my father borrowed enough money to buy Honeyneuk and a generation later there were new strangers wending their way in about the farm. This time they were not taxmen but mineral prospectors coming side by side with the oil explorers in the near-certain belief that there were commodities such as zinc to be found in that stretch of Buchan. Mysterious helicopters buzzed overhead with detecting equipment, to be followed by men with persuasive arguments as to why my father should sell away the exploration rights of his two hundred arable acres for an annual retainer.

But North-East independence or shrewdness or thrawnness or whatever you care to call it will not be swept aside by the first influx of oil and mineral men. The divining rights of his land were to stay with my matter-of-fact father, John Webster, who simply raised his verbal shotgun, as opposed to Willie Paul's metallic one, and fired a Buchan broadside which was no less effective. In a changing and perplexing world I would lay a pound to a penny that our highly individualistic North-East character will do more to change the oil industry than the oil industry will do to affect the character of the North-East.

So the destination of the northward journey had been reached in my native village of Maud, twenty-eight miles beyond Aberdeen and perhaps marked 'Maud Junction' if your map precedes the surgery of Doctor Beeching. But that is not an end. In the contermacious ways of a Buchan man, let me upset the English dictionary by saying that the destination is just the beginning of our story. . . .

Chapter Two

Mains's Wooin'

The Buchan area of Scotland is bounded roughly by the towns of Peterhead, Fraserburgh, Turriff and Ellon and takes in one of the most intensively cultivated corners of the world. The fact that that is so is a memorial to the generations of decent, hard-working folk who have bent their bodies in sweated toil because Buchan, in all honesty, is by nature a sour and grudging land which has been tamed and cleared and ploughed and manured and nursed into a state of fertility which makes it one of the great agricultural romances of all time.

Out of it has come a breed of folk who have forged their own character, a quietly industrious people who have learned the lesson of making the most of what you have in this world and accepting that things might be a damned sight worse. Their unfashionable philosophy, were it more widely applied by mankind, might put the world in better heart. Such people are often the salt of the earth, developing their own dogged charac-ter and dry sense of humour with which they survey the urban scene with its ostentations and softer ways and pass some fairly harsh, but perhaps realistic, judgments. With the toil of their own hands, as I remember it, they ran their crofts and small-holdings and looked westward to Deeside and the aristocratic half of Aberdeenshire with a measure of tolerant disdain for the inbred lairds and their tweedy wives who came visiting to shoot the grouse, stalk the deer and fish the salmon before returning to the well-padded comfort of Eaton Square.

I grew up in a Buchan which thought less of such people than of the man who worked his own bit place and the cottar who raised a big family to provide the labour of the fields. I grew up with the broad rhythms of the land, the parks and the peesies, the smell of hot dung rising from stubble braes that surrounded our village of Maud which lay at the centre of it all. One half of it lay in the Parish of New Deer and the other in the Parish of Old Deer, which seemed an appropriate and comfortable place for a lady like Maud to lie. Eastward from the heights of Bonny-kelly came the modest River Ugie which lapped its way round the village and ambled on between the historic Abbey of Deer and the hillside of Aikey Brae, which figures more prominently in the ramblings ahead. The valley blossomed out at Old Deer as the Garden of Buchan, for there at least you found an abundance of trees which were sadly absent from the rest of this highly-cultivated area.

Maud slumbered through each week till Wednesday when it stirred to become the biggest weekly cattle market in Britain, large floats careering down the country roads with load upon load of steaming livestock until you would think near all the beasts in Scotland were there, penned in the enclosures that stretched up and down the centre of the village, cattle lowing, sheep bleating and pigs skirling their various pleasures and protests. By ten o'clock the farmers had arrived in their hundreds, fine hardy chaps, ruddy from the exhilaration of outside work, puffing away at those short-stemmed Stonehives and greeting each other in twinkling but economic terms.

In the nineteen-thirties they came by bus and train and bicycle though today, with the trains removed and farming a more viable business, they flow in by motor car in an irregular progression which proves that, while they are perhaps the finest farmers in the world, they are without doubt the worst drivers. They seem to suffer from a curious notion that they have some kind of right of ownership to the public highway, particularly that half of it which comes in the opposite direction, and that perhaps explains the true story of the Buchan farmer who was charged with careless driving, having collided with another car while negotiating a local bend on the wrong side of the road. Scratching his head in puzzlement, he told the officiating policeman: 'Damnt tae hell, min, I've been gyan roon that corner the same wye for forty years an' I've never met anither car afore!'

The Wednesday morning scene would gain momentum, sharny-hipped bullocks and heifers, some fine and plump and some just shargers glad to be leaving the bareness of a sour croft, now driven on the hoof from nearby places, the fine rich smell of their bodies filling the nostrils with satisfaction. Less poetic roadmen who had to clean up afterwards said they were nothing but a skittery mess. As boys, we went down to the sale-ring and immersed ourselves in the babel of voices, farmers clustered round the arena, the blue-grey haze of cattle breath and Bogie Roll thickening in the shafts of sunlight which streaked in from roof windows. Through the fug it was just possible to pick out the auctioneer, rasping out his vocal short-hand from the rostrum, picking up winks and nods and veiled movements of the finger which were visible only to the sharp eye of experience. The man in the rostrum was my father, standing just where he had been when they brought him word one Wednesday morning that I had been born, a fact which was evidently absorbed with a perfunctory nod in the lull between a long-legged piner and a rough Irish stot.

The sale would continue well into the afternoon, with much coming and going of seedsmen and travellers and insurance lads till the attention which had been firmly fixed on pigs and stirks and farra coos was just as firmly transferred to the de-lights of Jimmy Henry's pub or the 'Refresh' at the railway station, which was run with maidenly care by the sisters Lil and Lena Murison. If the liquid lunch, which was always liable to extend beyond three courses, flowed out of control, a gig or hired Ford car was summoned to convey the casualty back to the farmstead. The Buchan farmer may not readily have admit-ted defeat but he had a special regard for John Barleycorn as a stiff opponent. Then the sun would stretch away across by Culsh, bringing the settled mellowness of late afternoon by which time the buses and trains had drained away the crowds, leaving our village and its five hundred inhabitants to relax

once more into that six-day slumber from which they would
surface next Wednesday and all the Wednesdays to come.

Life in a Scottish village before the Second World War was a
placidly settled existence, with a firm base of family roots
around the district and a predictable pattern of events in which
the pace of any change, were it there at all, would have
disturbed no-one. Everybody knew everybody else, from their
pedigree to their pets, which explains the concern of one dear
Buchan lady who was paying her first visit to London. In the
uncaring bustle of King's Cross Station she spotted a poor stray
cat and, turning to the relative who was meeting her, she
inquired: 'Noo, fa's catty would that be?' Back home in
Buchan it would not have been a ridiculous question.

Within that recognisable setting my own family tree had
taken root, a story which is told upon the gravestones of neighbouring parishes like Aberdour and Gamrie, where every one
of my forefathers for seven or eight generations had the name of
John Webster. Whatever they lacked in the originality of
choosing names they made good in honest toil. As the weavers
of the Macfarlane clan they must have tired of the webs and
turned instead to farming which had been their occupation for
two hundred years or more. Their testimony, like that of their
neighbours, lies in the fine arable lands of Buchan which they
coaxed to fruition. But their plodding peasantry is short of
drama, except for the extraordinary event of 1913, when my
father's father contracted the animal disease of anthrax from
one of his cattle and promptly died, leaving my father with the
job of running the smallholding at Backhill of Allathan, New
Deer, from the age of eight. Older men lent a neighbourly hand
and marvelled at the enterprise of the child. As well as sorting
the beasts he was soon working as a drover of cattle to the
market and setting his heart on the ambition of his life – to
occupy that rostrum in the mart at Maud. His aim was achieved
in his middle twenties, before I was born, and John Webster
grew in both girth and stature as perhaps the most sound and
sensible authority on the subject of Buchan farming. In the
absence of a proper schooling, he not only taught himself every-

thing from decimal fractions to land measurement but developed a gift for shrewd judgment which was close to uncanny, whether it concerned the quality of a beast or the honesty of a man. Embracing it all was a powerful personality which mixed great good humour with a ready temper and was fired by an engine room of energy which exhausted lesser mortals like myself, even in the observing of it.

He was well-built, with ruddy complexion and he embodied a talent for rural vulgarity which came so naturally that it caused little offence. He believed in calling a spade a bloody shovel and to hell with those who objected. His standard description of anything which was intolerably tough, for example, was to say that it was 'as hard as Hinnerson's erse' (Henderson's arse; Henderson being a North-East name for the Devil). If questioned on how hard 'Hinnerson's erse' was supposed to be, he would explain that it was ten times harder than flint, which surely made the point! If his pipe choked up and would neither suck nor blow he would fly into a rage at the confounded thing and declare that it was 'as ticht as a fisherman's erse – it'll naither let oot wind nor in water', which is just what a fisherman would need on a stormy sea!

As might be anticipated in such a man, the cultural realms of music, drama or literature were foreign fields into which he never ventured. The only concession he ever made to such wasteful pursuits was to give us a song which he learned at his mother's knee and which he intoned with a rare absence of anything resembling time, tone or rhythm. We would hide our amusement as he launched himself into his one and only song which went like this:

When I was a little wee pirn-taed loon
The ca'ed me 'silly little Jocky'
Ae day I was sittin' on ma granny's windae sill
Eatin' sweeties fae a grey paper pyokey

When by came a lassie and she offered me a kiss
I said 'That's a thing I never think o' scornin''

She bolted tae ma sweeties, ca'ed ma heid through the windae
And ma granny tellt me this neist mornin'

For it's aye said sayin' it's a bawbee for a bap
And a rosy-cheekit aipple aye lyin' on the tap. . . .

There ended the rendering, with a glow of pride that he had
made his contribution to culture, while remaining blissfully
unaware that the last verse was still two lines short of making
poetic sense.

In the balancing ways of nature, such a man will almost inevitably marry a woman of a wholly different type and so it was
with the ebullient John Webster, Buchan auctioneer. From the
farm of Whitehill, several miles away, he met Margaret Barron,
a fresh-faced country lass who harboured dreams of becoming a
ballet dancer, and though that world was impossibly out of her
reach in an Aberdeenshire backwater, she would pirouette and
caper about the house and bicycle cheerfully along country
roads with the wind blowing through her hair.

Her pedigree was not only different from that of John
Webster but a rather unusual one in the Buchan setting. She
was, in fact, descended from the family circle of Robert Burns,
Scotland's national bard, whose grandfather, Robert Burness
(that was the spelling) farmed at Clochinhill, near Stonehaven.
Robert Burness had a brother William, a neighbouring farmer,
from whom my mother was directly descended. Into that line
of breeding, just two generations before herself, came another
talented family, the Greigs, who claimed relationship with
Edvard Grieg, the national composer of Norway, whose family
was rooted at Rathen, near Fraserburgh, before his grandfather emigrated to Norway and changed the name from Greig
to Grieg. Unlike the Burns connection, I cannot produce proof
of a link with Edvard Grieg though the family themselves believed that they knew it. The focal point of the Greigs,
however, was my great-grandfather, Gavin Greig, born in
1856, the son of a forester at Parkhill Estate of Dyce, near
Aberdeen, a tall, lean and languid boy of great intellectual gift.

As dux of his school he had also shown great promise as a pianist, organist and composer and the time spent on these other interests brought him the shame of entering the University of Aberdeen as fourth bursar instead of first, which was his proper intellectual measure. In those days there was little choice for a lad o' pairts in rural Scotland so he became a teacher, at the age of twenty-two the headmaster of the modest country school at Whitehill in the parish of New Deer, just three miles up the road from Maud, and there he settled in a job well beneath his capacity but with plenty of spare time to devote to his first love, which remained music.

Even at the end of the last century there was a great wealth of folk song being handed down by word of mouth but Gavin Greig realised that the habit was dying and that a whole field of Scottish tradition would be lost for ever. So he undertook what was to be the main work of his life, that of preserving in proper form the folk songs of North-East Scotland. Night after night he would mount his bicycle and scour the countryside, hunting out old men and women who recalled to him the versions which had been handed down to them. Sometimes there would be a variation, different words, a slightly different tune. All were catalogued.

At the end of the night the man of the house would escort Maister Greig to the road-end and there perhaps he would remember a verse which had eluded him by the ingle-neuk. So down they would crouch by the fun-buss, with the man humming above the sough of the wind while Greig was feverishly jotting down words or musical notes by the light of a storm lantern. The tedious process went on for years. Published in the *Buchan Observer* in Peterhead and later in book form, it is counted as perhaps the greatest collection of its kind in existence, safely housed in the library of King's College in the University of Aberdeen.

Those who know more about it than I do will confirm that it is a work of quite remarkable achievement, painstaking and thorough in its research and brilliant in its final sifting and presentation. Folk song is a branch of musical and poetic expression which needs to be fed and nurtured from a great depth of natural root and not everything which has been handed on as the 'song of the folk' can be regarded as entirely authentic and trustworthy. Down the ages there is many an ambitious versifier who has tampered with the originals and superimposed his own ego upon the true ancestry of the work. Perhaps it can best be said of Gavin Greig that he combined genius with honesty, a mixture which readily conveys itself to the human instinct. As a result, scholars have come from as far as America to study his work, sometimes with a sense of hero-worship and a gaze of reverence for his descendants, some of whom are not much acquainted with the collection and merely blush at the reflected glory.

Of the large family circle, my cousin, Arthur Argo, who became a producer with the BBC, had acquired the closest affinity with the mood and spirit of our great-grandfather's work. Folk song, in fact, had a lean period but Arthur Argo, with his inherited interest, was there at the beginning of the modern revival. In 1961, while in his mid twenties, he had taken leave of absence from his job as a reporter on *The Press and Journal* to tour the clubs and campus lands of the United States with not much more than a toothbrush, a guitar and a good Scots tongue. In the rovings of his six-month adventure he gathered friends and admirers with names like Bob Dylan, whose legendary status was still in the future. Back home, Arthur was already playing his major part in a folk revival, befriending young lads like Billy Connolly and Gerry Rafferty, and becoming in his own day one of Scotland's leading authorities on the subject of folk music.

But if the folk-song fame of Gavin Greig was strong in foreign parts, his reputation in Scotland during his own lifetime rested more on another activity, the one inherited from the Burnsian strand of his ancestry. As well as being a fine musician he had a keen observation, a sense of the dramatic and a true feeling for words. So in 1894 he produced something for the stage in a form which was not too familiar at the time. It was a play with music, a rural saga of the lives and loves of country people, their trials and troubles and the beautiful simplicity of their days. He called it *Mains's Wooin'*. It captured the imagination of its day and has been produced by local companies in many a school and village hall throughout the twentieth century. In 1954 there was a diamond jubilee performance back in the parish of New Deer where it all started and the chairwoman on that memorable evening was none other than Nellie Metcalfe, who had been the beautiful leading lady of that first *Mains's Wooin'* exactly sixty years earlier. Nellie had become the wife of Archie Campbell, farmer at Auchmunziel of New Deer and a well-known columnist in *The Press and Journal* under the name of 'The Buchan Farmer'. Nellie herself had become a writer of more distinction than Archie and together they produced a daughter, Flora, who combined their talents and became in more recent times one of the best Scottish poets of her day, under her married name of Flora Garry.

The jubilee performance of *Mains's Wooin'* was followed in 1963 by a mammoth production in the natural outdoor setting of the countryside with a cast of hundreds, including massed choirs and orchestra; and proving that Gavin Greig had captured something of worth in his play, the country folk came flocking to see it in 1963 just as they had done in 1894, recognising some basic thread of rural life which endures when other superficialities have passed away.

Gavin Greig followed up with a sequel, *Mains Again* and then with perhaps his finest musical creation of all, the operetta *Prince Charlie*. But the 'Prince' was a lavish production and, although it ran for a week at a time in places like Peterhead, the costumes had to be hired from London and there was a limit to the number of local societies which could afford the expense. He also collaborated in such notable musical works as *The Harp and Claymore* with that most memorable of Scottish violinist-composers, his friend Scott Skinner, and wrote four novels as well as the poetry which is represented in Edwards *Modern Scottish Poets*.

In his introduction to Greig's poetry in 1884 (the poet was only twenty-eight) D.H. Edwards wrote: 'He is an accomplished musician as well as a tuneful and sweet poet, and although frequently urged to collect his scattered productions and issue them in book form, he has not as yet consented to do so. He looks on his poetical efforts as a mere mental recreation but the selections we give amply vindicate Mr Greig's right to be heard. His poetry is clearly the utterance of his heart. It is sustained by a sweet-toned fancy and is poured forth in natural gushes of feeling, clear and limpid as a Highland burn, and giving evidence of a rich mental poetical sympathy with the sights and sounds of nature.'

Gavin Greig was, of course, a product of the very soil from which the Buchan dialect of Scotland had sprung, not merely some intellectual who applied his curiosity to a quaint native speech but a man who had grown with it as naturally as the corn on the clay. His opening stanza on 'The Grampians' for example goes like this:

> Lat gentry chiels and ne'er-do-weels
> Gang owre the warld stravaigin'
> Syne rave an' write lang screeds o' styte
> O' foreign kintras braigin' –
> Het birstlin' clime, or realms o' rime,
> O' drouthy lands an' swampy anes;
> Here lat me bide nor budge a stride
> Frae Scotland and her Grampians

But his natural affinity with the Scots tongue did not hinder a brilliant command of the English language. His beautiful description of a Scottish Sabbath, written as a very young man, is too long to quote in full but you get the flavour of his mellow rhythms in the opening lines:

> It is the Sabbath morn; how still the day
> breaks on our native Scotland. Lo! it comes
> The deputy of Heaven, and freshly clad
> In all the mild authority of Peace.
> See how its advent chases every sight

17

and sound suggestive of the secular world. . . .

So he proceeds to paint a word picture of the country worshippers wending their way to the kirk in the graveyard, some sitting on table slabs till the parson arrives, leading them to the pews and to a psalm of David:

> O'er the pews
> a rustling wakes, as on a quiet noon
> a leafy beech tree shivers and is still;
> For each is turning to the psalm announced.
> That duly found, the people turn to mark
> What tune the slow revolving placard tells;
> Some ancient melody, of style severe,
> Their fathers sang in old reforming days.

Tall and delicate and wearing a slight stoop by the time he reached his middle years, Gavin Greig surrounded himself with a wide spectrum of friends at the Schoolhouse of Whitehill, playing the organ and talking with a fluency and wit that drew intellectuals from all over the country. Their delight in his company was matched only by their surprise that such a being should bury himself in the backwater of Whitehill. But that was where he now belonged, where he fathered his nine children and where he was as genuinely at home with the local farm servants as he was with the visiting professors from Edinburgh.

It is also where you will find old folks even today who will glow with idolatory at the mention of his name. Despite his many fringe activities, he was also hailed as one of the finest schoolmasters in the land, admired, respected and sometimes feared in a smoking cap which offset his long, droopy moustache and the glittering ring which shone from a lean, artistic hand. Such a man was not robust. *Angina pectoras* had raised its restless agony and the news that a great war was breaking upon the world aggravated his condition and depressed his spirit. He foresaw such an upheaval in the affairs of the human species that he could hardly bear the thought of it. He did not have to. For he died in the month it began, August of 1914, a brilliant Scot still in his fifties with a lot of useful work to complete.

Among the young men inspired by his work was Alexander Keith, an Aberdeen graduate who became assistant editor and chief leader writer of the *Aberdeen Daily Journal* after the First World War. In 1925 he edited the ballad portion of Greig's folk song collection, which was entitled *Last Leaves of Traditional Ballads and Ballad Airs*, described by a leading American critic as the best book of its kind in existence. Alexander Keith, whose journalism appeared under the initials A.K. and whose books included *A Thousand Years of Aberdeen*, had this to say of my great-grandfather in his introduction to the 'Last Leaves':

Had the accident of birth or the locality of his employment placed Gavin Greig within the notice of the London newspapers, there would be no need to write, at this date (1925), a tribute to his memory or to give an account of his research into popular poetry and the music of the people.

Like most studious men, quiet work excluded both the desire and the opportunity for self-advertisement.

As a recorder, especially of music, Greig was a master, for not only had he the knowledge of the art in very full degree, but he possessed also the extraordinarily percipient 'ear' which is sometimes, though by no means always, found in persons of high sensibility.

It is unfortunate that Greig did not reduce his conclusions into a complete and final judgment on the various problems of popular and traditional minstrelsy which cropped up to confront him during his investigations. Many of his theories were embodied in the lectures he delivered, some of which have been reprinted. But he had undoubtedly much more to say.

He carried his comments, as many a poor Scot had carried his library, 'under his bonnet' and death has obliterated the trace of them. Nevertheless, such opinions as he did commit to writing, combined with the range and interest of his collection, are proof of a remarkable penetration of research and soundness of reasoning.

So generously did he devote his strength and his abilities to his chosen subject that his epitaph may, not unjustly, be borrowed from Charles Murray's lines on the death of Heraclitus: —

'Death that coffins a' the lave, your sangs can never kist.'

In the tragic pattern of those days, death had coffined some of Gavin Greig's own children before himself. Little Nellie, aged twelve, had gone to Crimond to keep house for her married sister, Maggie, who lay dying from consumption. But the child was smitten by the galloping variety and had to be taken to her grave at New Deer just ahead of her sister. The folk of those days were protected by a faith which somehow cushioned them from the overwhelming heartbreaks they had to endure. Maybe the faith diminished with the apparent need for it but it has left us pretty vulnerable, has it not, in our modern society which has found no substitute in times of distress.

Chapter Three

A Buchan Sunrise

In the days of Gavin Greig it was the survival of the fittest, and the genetic strength of his breeding had come first. His eldest child, Edith, who became my grandmother, survived them all and reigned into her nineties as the grand duchess of the family circle. From the Schoolhouse of Whitehill she had married Arthur Barron, a local farmer who took over the tenancy of Mains of Whitehill, and there they lived a hard and demanding life, wresting a bare living for themselves and their five surviving children, of whom my mother, Margaret Barron, was the eldest.

So the ebullient John Webster took his bride to the hotel at the Howe of New Deer and married her on a day of ferocious gales. As the small group of relatives sat down to the feed, douce and ill at ease as folk tend to be at weddings, funerals and other disturbing events, old Granny Webster had the benefit of a clear view up the village brae when she startled the gathering by jumping to her feet and exclaiming that a cartload of straw had been blown right over, farmer and all. There was a general scampering to mount a rescue operation for Buchan folk are not of the sort to let the minor matter of a wedding come between them and lending a hand to a fellow creature in distress.

With such an inauspicious send-off, my father and mother began their married life in a but-and-ben which still stands as a ruin at Mill of Bruxie, two miles from Maud, a place so riddled with vermin that my father spent his spare moments shooting rats from the kitchen window. By the time I was born they had moved to another two-roomed house at Fedderate Cottages in the village of Maud and it was there, in the front room, that I first saw the light of day on Wednesday, 8 July, 1931, a grand day to be born, folk said, though, despite a certain talent for recall, I am forced to admit that the experience escapes me!

By the time I was three we had moved into the more modern comfort of a council house at 2 Park Crescent and that was where my childhood came into its own. My father's personality as well as his job created a certain vortex of activity so it was a busy household with much coming and going of farm folk and martmen, everything leading up to the climax of the Wednesday mart then running down to the trough of the weekend and back up again. Dad went off to canvass for cattle at Fraserburgh on a Tuesday, while Fridays were spent in Aberdeen, where he auctioned at the mart's headquarters at Kittybrewster. The rest of his week was taken up with visits to Buchan farms to solicit cattle for the Wednesday mart, to arrange a displenish sale for farmers who were moving or a letting of grass for those with pasture to spare. In those early days there were three separate auctioning companies in the village of Maud, all competing for the livestock which would pass through their salerings. The two major companies were the Central and Northern Farmers Mart and the family firm of Reith and Anderson, neither of whom paid over-much attention to the minor competition from another family concern, which was Middleton's Mart. Indeed when my father became auctioneer to Middleton around 1930 he was sometimes struggling to muster six cattle for his Wednesday sale as against the massive numbers of his two big rivals. There was no contest. But he scoured the countryside on his motor-bike, seeking to establish himself as an honest man who knew something about beef cattle and was willing to learn the rest. Some bigsy farmers gave him short shrift and treated him rather shamefully but a few kindly men recognised his worth and good intentions and helped him to build up a clientele for Middleton's Mart. Week by week his figure rose till he became a major threat to the two big firms and brought himself a new respect among folk who knew the business. In time the three mart companies amalgamated and my father ended up as manager of the combined operation at Maud, never forgetting to return his thanks to the farmers who had given him a helping hand in those struggling days at Middleton's; and if the truth be known, he never quite forgot the ones who belittled him either.

All the time he was dispensing advice and help which became more and more eagerly sought by those who had learned of his instinct for a sound decision. All men were equal in my father's eyes and sometimes he would spot an able farm servant and encourage him to take the lease of a small croft as the first step on the road to becoming a farmer. The poor chap would shrink from lack of confidence but Dad would steel his nerve and offer him his first few cattle which did not have to be paid until they were brought back for sale, having been fattened to the butchers' requirements. Many a prosperous farmer to this day harks back to the time that my father bullied him into accepting the responsibility. He seldom had a failure. Widows or spinster ladies left to run a family holding would turn to him for help in stocking the place with cattle. One such lady, Miss Oliphant from Tyrie, was eternally grateful for his wise counsel. She was also distressed one day to learn that he had been laid low with measles and was in fact lying beside his pale-faced, seven-year-old son, a fearsome spectacle by contrast with a round red face resembling a harvest-moon and covered in a most comical mass of scarlet spots. Father and son were feeling deeply miserable together when the morning post brought the sympathetic note from Miss Oliphant. I can still recall the occasion as he opened the letter and read it out in his deliberate, matter-of-fact tones: 'Dear Mr Webster; I am very sorry to hear that you are in bed with a measle . . .' The rest was lost in an explosion of oaths. 'A measle?' exclaimed my rumbustious father. 'Ah've thoosans o the buggers!'

Meanwhile my mother would busy herself about the house, making cups of tea for Johnnie Ingram, the martman who would come hopping in with all the bounce of a bantam-cock, or Andra Forbes, the village bobby, who put his head cautiously round the sick-room door, gaped in amazement at the sight of my father's much-measled face and exclaimed 'Goad, what an ugly bugger!' before retreating in haste to a safer distance. Mam would conduct the business of the mart by means of the new-fangled contraption called the phone, which had recently come along to intrude on domestic privacy while giving you a certain exclusiveness in the village community; for it was not everybody who had a phone, was it? Even then she was struggling with chronic bronchitis which she used to describe rather graphically as having the taste of 'roosty nails'. She longed for the opportunity 'tae gyang doon wi' a barra and spad an' hae a gweed redd-oot.' (Translated from the Buchan dialects that means: 'to go down with a barrow and spade and have a good clean-out.')

But she was a brave and cheerful spirit and when the measles had subsided she and I would value the times when my father with his more oppressive ways was out of the house and we could turn on the wireless at high volume and cavort to the mellow tones of Harry Roy, Henry Hall, Roy Fox, Ambrose or Jack Hylton. At the same time my father was graduating from an old, dickie-backed car with a running-board and an outside battery to a green Austin 12 with the registration of RG 6502, which sticks with me to this day, when I would be incapable of telling you the number of my current car! In such new-found comfort we managed to drive to Glasgow for the Empire Exhibition of 1938, the biggest event ever held in Scotland, and there we found ourselves lodgings in Copland Road, just opposite Ibrox Park, and spent our days among the wonders of that spectacular show in Bellahouston Park. A miniature train transported you round the vast acreage of pavilions, which portrayed the life of the British Empire, and when the evenings came and the fountains and waterfalls were lit up in colour and the gigantic tower on the hill went soaring into the night sky, the crowds would link arms and dance up and down the terraced steps to the craze of the moment, which was 'The Lambeth Walk'. The effect on the child mind was inspirational. While in Glasgow for that first time, we joined a boat excursion to Clydebank and sailed round the hull of a massive ship which my mother explained would soon be sailing the high seas as the *Queen Elizabeth*. Thirty-five years later I was to commission a boat in Hong Kong Harbour to take me out to the bay where I sailed round that same ship, alas by then lying on her side, sabotaged and burned out in a heartbreaking spectacle. I had followed the great lady from her cradle at Clydebank to her graveyard in Hong Kong. On that occasion in 1938 we also visited Burns's Cottage at Ayr, feeling something of a family right to be there, and returning to Maud with a sense of having been on a world adventure. For travel was not the fashion of the day, except for those who went off to foreign parts and maybe never came back again. Anyone who had been abroad and returned was deserving of that curious interest which was later accorded to men who had been to the moon. Such creatures fell into two main categories: schoolteachers who had the time and the money to go during the long summer holidays and the ex-Servicemen who had been to France during the First World War. (It is now impossible to find a First War veteran who is under eighty and I find it sobering that I can remember them in their thirties.) A third category, almost beyond comprehension, had been policemen in faraway places like Shanghai or Hong Kong or tea-planters in Sumatra and some would come home with fine romantic tales of the East. But not all succeeded in making the impression they intended. One local adventurer home from his wanderings was holding court in the pub one night, extolling the benefits of travel as a means of broadening the mind and chastising the locals for their lack of enterprise. 'Be like me,' he counselled. 'Get out of this God-forsaken hole and see a bit of the world.' Old Geordie Bendie beheld him for a minute then said: 'Weel ye ken, Lord John Sanger had a circus and in the circus there was an ass. Lord John Sanger took his circus a' roon the world an' the ass went too. But when the circus came back, the ass was still an ass....' As the locals shuffled their feet and chuckled quietly, a pompous gent was finishing his drink more quickly than he intended and making for the door in a huff!

So life in a Scottish village took on its own pace and pattern and the filterings of it are still strong with me now. In the wet plap of winter I can hear the early-morning rattle of bottles, with milk-boys whistling out of tune, an extra pint for Mrs Fyte; still dark with only a threatening glimmer of light in the east; now an early horse led by eident crofter was whinneying at the smiddy door and Willie Ogston handled it to a stall and gripped a hoof between his legs, having forged a shoe in a shower of sparks and cooled it in a sizzle of cold water. Then the day broke open and roadmen boarded a Leyland lorry to quarry stone from Aikey Brae. Country bairns, fresh from three-mile walks and shaming village laziness, came dysting in with piece-bags, fine ruddy cheeks and burning lugs well primed to hear the good sense of the three R's before returning to sort nowt and to bed themselves down on chaff. As the frosts came creeping up the howe, laying their crisp sparkle over ploughed park and grass, braeside croft or village dell, it was time for Christmas, tinsel wonder and kirk bells tolling for a simple service with candles and a fine warm feeling of neighbourliness and comfort and sureness. And as the snowdrift came creeping in the wake of the blast it was time to sledge clear parallel lines on virgin snow, fine moonlit nights with gay young voices echoing on distant hills then panting home, well past the hour, to the joys of deep sleep and the morning sorrow of thaw and brown slush, sandy water choking in the gurgle of drains, making a fair sotter of wonderland. Soon fresh winds were sweeping through the howe, clearing the last vestige of speckled white from the lithe of dykes; and days were waxing into Spring, the twitter of birds, bairns out to play beyond teatime and the bleat of a paraffin tractor telling of furrows that were spared the blast of winter and were only now folding over, one upon the other, in the neat harmony of Spring soil.

As crops were sown, a new crop of human flesh went fleet-footed to the excitement of Miss Catto's infant class, a world begun, of plasticine and counting beads, the smell of chalk and rubber and fresh exercise books, of slate and a one-third pint of morning milk and the exquisite reward for a week of diligent application – the Friday afternoon caramel. Simple days, simple tastes, lullabies and tender stirrings of love. Then the sun came higher in the sky and nights stretched through April and May to a sniff of summer that brought June on its wing, warm, steaming soil pushing up shoots of corn. June that brought holidays from school, an eternity that ended, sultry days of thunder-clapping and bursting rain and sun again and steam and cattle shows with animal breath and smell of skin and sharn, with crowds gathered at the ringside cheering hammer-throwers and Highland dancers, lustily taking sides in the embedded battles of tug o' war; great brosey chiels with names to terrify and at the end of the line an anchor-man of enormity, lying sodden with rope bound round his shoulders, determined not to yield an inch. The Bell family was the big name, all brothers and cousins from Tyrie, near Fraserburgh, welded into a leaden mass of brute force, heaving and checking to the command of their family head, Alex Bell, an auctioneer like my father and an irresistible force of heavyweight proportions, though short in the leg, filling the local church with as powerful a bass voice as there was in the land.

As the show days wore late the drunks were havering and slavering and tumbling in a world that would not stand still; the fiddles were tuning up for the marquee dance. Shy young deems and bolder ones, unable to get to the show during the day, came biking in from byre and bigging to cast themselves incautiously into the spinning-wheel of the Eightsome Reel, the Quadrilles or the Lancers, with hulking chiels fresh from hammer-throwing or whisky tent birling them off their feet, skirts flying out to uncover thighs of fiery flesh, an unco sight to blind the timid. The music and the heat and sweat and smoke fermented in a heady night that tailed off behind dykes and trees and left tired limbs for milking the kye or cutting the corn. And the golden rustle of hairst was here, binders whirring their tunes of glory, spilling out sheaves that were stookit and left to dry in the late summer winds. Horse and cart were yokit in a week or two, neighbours came to help with the leading, stooks were forked on to the carts and led to the corn-yard where Grandpa's undisputed eminence as a ruck-builder with the eye of an artist came into its own. Rucks were thackit and tied against the wind and with the fields bare of all but stubble the triumphant cry of 'Winter!' went up and that was what was now awaited. The great joy of helping in the fields at hairst time was the arrival of the kitchie deem with the 'piece,' the kettle of tea with the baps or plain loaf brought up from Morrison's Bakery and spread with home-made butter and syrup or raspberry jam (how much better does a mug of tea taste in the great outdoor, especially as a relief from hard toil). Then October winds blew cold and the long summer nights that had the sun no sooner ducking down than he was bobbing up again became long hours of darkness, with the great furnace shining his excesses on Australia and places like that with little wish for him. In the grey autumn, Granny Barron took the child on her knee and amused with rhymes like:

> Chin cherry
> Mou' merry
> Nose nappy
> E'e winky
> Brow Brinky
> Ower the hill and awa tae stinky!

Whatever the sense, it never failed to amuse and she prodded her tongue in the child ear to heighten the climax. So we were back in the trauchle of dub and drudgery, grey dreich days that passed with a 'Losh aye, man, fairly that' or a spit or a quiet laugh. And the milk bottles rattled in the village doorways and the loons were whistling 'Red Sails in the Sunset'. But aye, there was a warm fireside.

Chapter Four

Philosophy and Fags

The trouble with the fireside of the nineteen-thirties was just that it resided in the kitchen or the living-room and on cold and frosty days and nights the rest of the house was fit for few but Eskimoes. How we survived in those days before central heating remains one of the lingering mysteries of my childhood. Mothers, being the dog's-bodies of the rural home, invariably got up first and lit the fire to bring some semblance of warmth before the rest of the family stirred. Yesterday's paper laid the foundation for a criss-crossing of kindlers and a mixed crowning of coal and cinders and if the confounded thing went out, as it usually did, you splashed it with paraffin which fairly made the lum rumble in a roar of flame and maybe set fire to the soot, sending a shower of red sparks and black yoaming reek to torment an early-morning washing. The dry lavvies which were often situated discreetly at the bottom of the garden were giving way to bathrooms in my young day but that was still a mixed blessing when a visit for the simplest call of nature meant that you ran a high risk of developing icicles where icicles were never meant to be. Undressing for a bath was such a nightmare that many people didn't bother. If the truth were known, many a country body of my acquaintance went through a whole lifetime without ever experiencing the shock of total immersion. Some took the view that even if cleanliness did come next to Godliness, there was no need to extend the thing to madness. In any case, a film of good clean dirt was maybe nature's best protection from germs, folk said, setting the invisible creatures to fight each other and leave a body in peace and good health. But there was one occasion at least when the feet, if no more, had to be solemnly washed and that was the night before you went to Aberdeen for the day – 'just in case you get knocked doon wi' a tramcar and land in the infirmary,' your mother would say. 'It wid be an affa disgrace if you had fool feet.'

My father, who was seldom stuck for a solution, had his own particular way of combatting the cold houses before the Second World War and indeed it was not an unusual one. He simply slept in a big thick semmit, his shirt, long woollen drawers and socks, which would have armoured him for the Antarctic and became such a habit that he saw no good reason for abandoning it in the hottest night of summer. As a child I wore 'combies', short for combinations, uniting woollen vest and pants in a garment which buttoned up the middle. To keep away colds we were fitted out with iodine lockets round our necks, totally unaware in those days that we were exposing ourselves to the dangers of radiation. When it came to maintaining good health, however, Dad always believed that nothing much would come over you if you kept your bowels open and your mind easy. It was his panacea for all ills and he did not hesitate to say so, couching it in terms which were as graphical as they were unprintable! He backed up his theory with splendid example, paying at least two and sometimes three visitations upon the private room every morning before leaving the house. He swore absolutely by the power of prunes and rhubarb.

But if we thought we were short of comfort in a village house it did us good to visit the farmhouses of the day which seemed pretty bare places in which to live. Red ochre walls, paperless and featureless and lit by a bleak paraffin lamp brought little cheer to folk who had bent their backs in toil from early light till darkness. Up at Mains of Whitehill the peat fire was the focal point of the evening, its shadows dancing on the walls with ghostly effect. Grandpa Barron would sit reading his books, poetry and dirt like that, folk said, and no one cared to speak unless they were spoken to. My uncle Arthur would sit cutting out paper shapes of horses and a most capital job he made of it too, him in his waistcoat and flannel shirt with stud but no collar; uncle Gavin would shave from a mug by the small mirror on the kitchen wall, scraping away a lather of soap with a cut-throat razor and revealing long furrows of bare skin with the same artistry that he would plough the stubble fields.

But the silent authority of Grandpa Barron belied the true heart of the man. Tall and studious, he had followed farming because it was the tradition and, through tradition, a passion of the blood, so he was a farmer by instinct. He tended his acres with motherly care, made two straws grow where one grew before and raised his children with love and discipline. I used to walk out with him from the farmhouse at Whitehill, through the dubby close to the bottom of the garden wall and there I would gaze up at him as he gazed out across his parks, his corn and his turnips, his grass and his cattle. There was a wistful look in his eyes which set me wondering what his thoughts might be. But they were private and sacred and not for the fathoming of a child. On occasion he would turn his hand to the writing of poetry and folk who read it and understood said it was grand stuff; fegs, the man shouldn't have been a farmer at all. Maybe his thoughts were of the life that might have been; then again they may have been his satisfied reflections on the life that existed, the real throbbing life of the land with its rhythmic pattern and pace, the golden corn stretching to the horizon by Hillies, broken only by the patchwork greenery of grass and neeps and the silver burn and the black stots. I think my grandfather perceived in his surroundings the basis of man's contentment, accepting the drudgery of the land as his price for living so close to the wonders of nature, privileged to a daily contact with God's own acre of poetry which was there for all to see and hear and smell.

Those visits to Whitehill were a particular joy, though my natural fondness for people and bustle brought a sense of the loneliness of country life when I went there for any length of time in the summer. Granny Barron would pad across the farm close with basins of milk in her hand and clods of boots on her feet, laced through hooks. One hook would catch on another and a piercing yell of 'Gweed preserve's!' would herald a slow-motion sprawl among the dubs, the milk overflowing in a tidal wave and streaking off as little white veins in a multitude of directions. Not that she was ever hurt for Providence takes care of drunk men, bairns and hapless grannies. In the hot sing of summer the smell of the farmyard, its hay and hen's dirt, the whirr of the cricket and the strut of the cockerel and the warm peace of the steading were a symphony of sight and sound to the soul of a child. Granny took pride in a self-confessed stupidity, on the basis that she didn't have enough sense to worry, a condition which served her well in a lifetime which stretched for more than ninety years, conscience-free and contented. Grandpa just supped his sowens and pease-brose and taught me to break oatcakes into a bowl of milk for what we called 'milk-and-breid' and, believe me, there was nothing finer.

In the loneliness of the farmstead the sight of a visitor was a matter of some excitement, though the only guarantee in the course of a day was the postman for, even if he had no letters, he would come pushing his bicycle up the road to deliver the Aberdeen *Press and Journal*, the daily paper of the North-East which brought all the local news. Every few weeks a fisher-wife would appear on the horizon with a creel on her back, a funereal figure in black dress and black shawl and smelling of kippers and yellow fish. These hardy souls came in family successions till their offspring were well known to the country customers. My granny knew the whole background of one particular fishwife and knew too that her daughter was expecting a child. Inquiring if the baby had arrived yet, she became engaged in the following conversation which is often recalled for amusement within our family:

Fishwife: Oh aye she got her bairn
Granny: And what did she ca' it?
Fishwife: She ca'ed it Barty.
Granny: Oh, she ca'ed it Barty?
Fishwife: Aye, she ca'ed it Barty. But she might as well hae ca'ed it Farty for it's deid!

PHILOSOPHY AND FAGS

In the summer evenings folk would bicycle up the farm road and into the close for a game of croquet on the farmhouse green and they would play into the gloaming, tying white handkerchiefs on the hoops to guide a ball through the gathering darkness. They were evenings which swung from serious concentration to laughter and good fellowship but how strange that such an English game as croquet should have flourished in rural Scotland. Yet flourish it did and there were some devastating performers to prove it, not least Uncle Gavin and Aunt Betty who swung a mallet as some people swing a golf club.

When the hairsting was over it was time for the meal-and-ale, with all the folk who had neighboured to each other gathering to sup at a bowl of the strong stuff, a fine robust way to round off the in-gathering of the crop. Sometimes they would dance in the corn-loft or just adjourn to the parlour (it was always 'the parlour' on Scottish farms) to enjoy a musical evening which was as much home-made as the meal-and-ale. In the dim light of a paraffin lamp or the brighter glow of the new-fangled Tilley, and with peat reek yoaming up the lum, Uncle Gavin fitted his great clods of hands over the keyboard of the piano and drew out as sweet an *arpeggio* as a concert pianist, giving little hint that these same hands had been riving at frosty neeps or clearing a strang-hole not long before. Gavin's natural talent was unspoiled by tuition and you will find him, even today, still playing for the Macduff Strathspey and Reel Society, though his sight has now all but gone. Meanwhile Uncle Arthur would be tuning up his fiddle, joined by a cacophony of people from surrounding farms who had brought along their fiddles too. Aunt Betty gave a bit tootle on her flute and soon the general disorder was brought to a halt as my grandfather intoned from his favourite corner of the fireside: 'Weel lads, fit aboot "Stumpy"?' And away they went, a full-blooded orchestra cramped into the parlour of a farmhouse, swinging into strathspeys and reels and old-fashioned waltzes, the lilting melodies of the hills and howes and mosses, clear as the crystal of the burn, pure as the gold of the corn that had just been cut from the fields. One tune followed another, interpolated with the

33

songs of Robbie Burns (we never called him Rabbie) or a more recent recitation from the North-East poet called 'Hamewith', whose real name was Charles Murray from Alford. There was a stop for a cup of tea and a dram then on again till the hour was late and the players exhilarated but exhausted. Then coats were fetched from the bedroom and the gas-lights were adjusted on bicycles before they set out upon their various directions, some in motor cars that had to be cranked with a starting-handle, and there was a final 'Gweednicht, folk, it's been a gran' affair' and my grandparents would call 'Hist ye back!' And back they would come on many another evening of joy and friendship.

Arthur and Gavin slept in the chaumer, which was normally the bothy of the work-folk, attached to the steading. They were typical of the farmers' sons who stayed at home to work if they were any use. If they weren't, they tended to be sent away to the agricultural college to take a diploma or a B.Sc. and to land in some advisory job with advice which their old father could no doubt have offered in the first place. One is reminded of Bernard Shaw's remark that 'he who can, does – he who cannot, teaches', though both Mr Shaw and myself are being a little facetious about a noble profession!

The wireless had not yet reached Mains of Whitehill so Granny and Grandpa travelled down to Maud to hear the broadcast funeral service of King George V when he died in 1936. They sat at the fireside and marvelled at the scientific wonders of the live transmission. My, whatever would they think of next? By the following year the conversation was dominated by talk of Edward VIII and a Mrs Simpson and folk were sharply divided. Some praised the uncrowned king for putting love before all else while others said he was simply under the infatuating influence of a bold hussy from America, a divorcee at that, who was clever in all respects except in her belief that the British people would accept her as queen. It was mostly above my head at the time, except that I had glossy picture books of Edward, Prince of Wales, and can still remember the linseed smell of the covers. His name was one of many which floated beyond the tide of understanding. Folk spoke about the Labour man, Ramsay MacDonald, and said 'A servant's bairn from Lossiemouth as Prime Minister? Lord, no wonder the world's in a mess!' They glowed with admiration and affection for Robert Boothby, a dashing young man with a shock of black hair who had exchanged the dust of Oxford for the sharn of East Aberdeenshire to sit him down in the House of Commons. And with growing alarm they talked about Hitler but that seemed far away and beyond my comprehension. I was safely cocooned within the gentle slopes which rose from the cavity of Maud and gave a microcosmic impression of the horizons of the world. I could encompass it all from a fence which overlooked the railway station, knowing for certain that England was down there beyond the Den Wood and that France lay just over the Hill o' Jock. Apart from England, France was the only foreign country I had heard anything about. Every 11 November we gathered in the gym hall of Maud School and bowed our heads in remembrance of men and things we knew not of. War, they said, the Somme and Ypres and Passchendale and I could only form my own imaginary picture of a clump of trees, like the one on top of Banks Hill, with men on horseback charging to a gory death.

Somebody said Amen and it was milk time, with cardboard top and a hole for the straw, then out we went to play tackie or cock-fighting and thought no more of the men and their war and their dying. Maud was my island, a self-contained paradise on which the few intrusions included the *Chick's Own* on a Tuesday and the *Dandy* on a Friday. When the adventures of Rupert became too juvenile then Korky the Cat became the fashion, while Desperate Dan convinced us that nothing was impossible. Hungry Horace was a kindred spirit, stuffing himself with all the things that were still available before wartime rationing. If Horace had stayed in Maud he would have been a regular customer of Lizzie Allan's sweetie shop, for Lizzie was the arch-priestess of the lollipop, goddess of gastronomy, who extracted the wonders of the world from secret holes of her poky little shop which was lit by a paraffin lamp that stank in every nostril. She was the magician whose wand could whip up an ecstatic galaxy of Mars and Milky Way, Aero, Sherbet and Cow Candy, striped balls and black-sugar straps. And Lizzie had no legs, not a toe to call her own. From early childhood two stumps had been her meagre standpoint but Nature, in the way that Nature does, paid compensation in the shape of a brilliant mind. She had had time to read and think and, legs or no legs, she had been able to travel to London in her younger day, wheeling her chair on to the guard's van of the King's Cross express, so that she could mix in the circle of sprouting Socialism.

In later years I was to discover that she dispensed politics with peppermints, philosophy with fags, never yielding a principle in the cause of business. Indeed, her main customers were the farmers on a Wednesday, buying their weekly supply of sweeties and tobacco, yet she would lash them for their wartime subsidies and fine motor cars and they would go away cursing 'that bloody Communist', determined that they would never darken her door again. But Lizzie, the reluctant capitalist, survived for more than forty years in that miserable shop and despite her enlightenment and visions of the future she never did concede to the comforts of electricity and modern living. She worked and slept in her shoppie, moving around in one of those old-fashioned basket wheelchairs which she pushed by the direct drive of her powerful arms. One day a crowd of mischievous youths were standing outside her shop when Tom Ogston joked to the others: 'I'll gyang in and tickle Lizzie's big tae.' Lizzie overheard and brought blushes by calling out: 'Come away in then, Tom, and have a try.' She was a noble spirit, a woman of wit and wisdom who bore her burden with a fine dignity. She had little time for religion, subscribing only to Shaw's idea of a life force, and expected to pass her eternity in oblivion. But for once she may have been wrong. I find it hard to believe that Lizzie Allan is not somewhere among the politics and the peppermints, even today, lecturing on the follies and fickleness of mankind, wearing the brown beret which was her companion for forty years and lighting a paraffin lamp at eventide . . . so that the good folk may see.

PHILOSOPHY AND FAGS

Lizzie was an essential part of our village scene, a vital thread in the pattern of permanency that gave us roots and a settled outlook on the world. Across the road from her wee shoppie in Timmer Street, Morrison the Baker made baps and butter biscuits (we called them 'hardies') which were unsurpassed in all the kingdom, while Chalmers the Baker along the street had his own distinctive delicacies. Down at the Square, Henry Panton the Saddler made harness for the horses and mended the canvas sheets for the harvest binders which cut the corn; John Grant the Miller ground your oats, Willie Ogston shod the horse, John Craig would mend your burst pipes, Hector Mavor was your joiner and told fine stories of his days in Chicago; Bob Sangster combined the skills of watchmaker and cycle agent and peered through his eye-glass surrounded by dozens of acid containers which were the wet batteries of the old wireless sets, in for charging; Alex Marshall delivered your coal but also obliged if you needed a hire, a hearse or a haircut.

Lizzie Allan surveyed it all from the confines of her wooden shop and kept up a fascinating range of conversation as she wheeled her solid torso from tobacco tin to sweetie jar, calling for the assistance of the customer only when the wanted item was totally out of her reach. I used to visit her every day, if only for my mother's regular packet of Players, which sold at 11½d for 20 (slightly less than 5p in today's money) and stood side by side on the shelf with Gold Flake, Capstan, Kensitas, Du Maurier and the black cat of Craven A, not to mention the more modest Woodbine which could be bought in little paper packets of five. I learned a lot from Lizzie and once asked her to jot down a few recollections of earlier days in our village. Her short scribble came to light in a recent rummage through my old trunk and this is what she wrote:

In the early days the Market Stance, which I can see from my back window and is now covered with cattle pens, was an open meadow with lovely green grass right up to the cross-roads. Johnny Still, the martman, kept everything nice and trig. Even the dungheap had a classical look, so square and even. In the spring, when the farmers came with their carts to drive it away, I regretted seeing it disturbed. The grass was damaged and for a time the place looked untidy but Nature soon covered the scars and beauty reigned again.

Every summer people camped on the Stance. I have seen a dozen horse-drawn caravans at one time and it was fascinating to watch them draw in, select a site and settle down. The Market Stance was considered common ground at that time so they had plenty of freedom and made themselves at home. Horses and dogs were all over the place. They usually arrived in June but the height of their season was a week or two before Aikey Fair in July. They generally did their cooking on oil stoves but sometimes they formed a circle of stones and made a fire, over which they cooked a big pot of mystery which was dished out to the various members of the clan when they came back from their day's outing.

The men generally set out with shalt and float, taking a scythe as well. They brought back a load of grass, cut from the roadside, to feed their horses and sometimes they brought heather, which they fashioned into scrubbers. Meanwhile the women had set off with baskets on their arms to peddle their wares around the countryside. I remember especially one woman who could neither read nor write and who came in to me every year and got me to write out an order to a firm in Aberdeen. She listed all the goods and the price per dozen or gross and always she could tell me to within a few coppers what the cost of the order amounted to.

Then there was old Betty Townsley who wore an outsize in gold ear-rings. When she came in for half-an-ounce of tobacco she called down so many blessings on my head that I felt quite embarrassed. But we seldom have any gypsies in the village now. There is little room left for them to camp.

Another feature of village life which has gone is the feeing markets and I don't think anyone regrets their passing. The one held in May was not too bad as the weather was warmer but the one in November was a day to be endured. In order to keep warm the farm lads visited the whisky booths pretty freely, with the result that they were soon full of spirit in more senses than one. Many and varied are the arguments I have heard from my back window when the boys got het-up. Sometimes it was about who had the best 'pair' or who kept the cleanest harness or sometimes they had a heart-to-heart chat about the merits or faults of a lady they alluded to as 'the deem'.

I did not like the feeing markets. It seemed such a crude way of engaging a servant and at the end of the day there were many who were still not fixed up. They could do nothing to help themselves unless they joined the army, and the Gordon Highlanders pipe band was always in attendance to show what a glamourous life it was. Wright's Amusements or some other shows were always here for the market and at night the local people got a thrill from trying their luck at hoop-la or the shooting gallery whilst the children enjoyed the swings and merry-go-rounds or pestered their parents to knock down a coconut.

Something else which belonged to the past and lent a rustic air to the village was the number of little dairies in our midst – Kitchenhill, the Temperance Hotel, Mary Lamb, Bob Wallace, Andrew Hendry and others who kept a few cows – and in the summer evenings it was pleasant to watch them meandering along the village streets to the byres from nearby grazing. A little later you saw the housewives with their milk pails going along to their favourite source of supply and, while waiting for the milk to be measured, they had a fine opportunity to exchange any tit-bit of gossip they had gathered during the day. The village pump also served the same useful purpose. Now modern hygiene has swept away the little dairies and, with running water in most homes, it almost seems that the only outlet left to the ladies for a friendly chat is the W.R.I.

I greatly regret the disappearance of the horses which used to be seen on our roads. It was pleasant to hear the clip-clop of their hooves when the farmers drove into the village on market day. They were a stout people, the old farmers of a generation back; there they sat perched high on the seat of the gig with nothing to protect them from the wind or rain, although some did sport a luggit bonnet or a gravat in winter. On they passed with a wave of the whip and a cheery greeting to friends. After the horse had been stabled they joined their friends in the bar and had a glass of whisky to stimulate the circulation of their blood. And if, in the course of the day, a farmer overdid it with business drams, why worry? After the horse was yoked, friendly hands helped him into his seat, put the reins in his hands and, once headed for home, the horse took charge and delivered him safely to his family.

A winter scene I liked to watch from my window was that of the bakers loading a sledge when the roads were blocked with snow and vans could not get through. They started away early and always took a shovel in case they got stuck in a drift, also a flour-sack in which to carry bread to any farmhouse where the roads were too bad for the sledge to reach. I can still picture Jimmy Morrison, muffled up in a heavy coat, stamping around, flapping his arms and giving vent to his feelings with a few seasonable oaths. When these men set off amidst the falling snow I felt they were akin to Arctic explorers.

Thus, in the early nineteen-fifties, Lizzie Allan was putting down some of her memories of an earlier part of the century, intended for publication in *The Maud Review*, a magazine I had founded in my boyhood as a first outlet to the journalistic urge. Several of the features which cropped up in Lizzie's narrative were still very much in vogue within my own memory of the thirties. As well as genuine gypsies and hawker people, cart loads of tinkers would pass through the village, stop off for a drink and perhaps start a fight in the heat of the whisky. As boys we gathered to watch the fracas, secretly excited by the prospect of some dreadful deed, but when it happened, with gory consequences, we ran for our lives lest the tinkers should close ranks and turn on us. There were poor bairns wrapped in shawls and sheltered by drunken women in the corner of miserable carts and one day the fighting factions charged off over the hill and down Broonies Brae, chasing each other with cries of vengeance. In the rabble and heat of the drink, a piner horse went over the dyke, taking cart and tinkers, women and bairns as well, and God knows what was the outcome.

Sometimes on a Saturday my parents would take me to the first house of the pictures at the Regal or the Playhouse in Peterhead, not that my father had much time for such doubtful pursuits. The talkies had arrived about the year I was born and the novelty had not worn off. Charlie Chaplin and Laurel and Hardy were still the rage, closely followed by Deanna Durbin's singing, Fred Astaire's dancing and Sonja Henie's skating. A band would play *Alexander's Ragtime Band* and the newsreel showed Amy Johnson flying across some distant water. *Snowwhite and the Seven Dwarfs* was a major event and when the picture was over we walked along the road to Luigi Zanre's for fish and chips to eat on the journey back to Maud. Somewhere about Mintlaw I would fade away, crunching at my second last chip, and hear only a half-world of adult voices and chugging engine till I was transferred to a warm bed, absorbing the mysteries and glamour of the Hollywood dream factory into the sub-conscious stream. But the talkies were not the only innovation of the thirties in our part of the world. All-in wrestling sprung into favour and every fortnight carloads of men would head off for Aberdeen to watch this or that grisly creature throwing his weight around the Music Hall. My father was caught up in the enthusiasm and came home with weird tales of a monster called Ali the Wicked, a fierce-looking Oriental who began his antics by praying towards Mecca before proceeding to commit all but murder, if the gyrations were to be taken as anything more serious than the comical gymnastics which they have certainly become in more recent times. At home I was fascinated by the one-man band who used to pass our way. With drum at his foot, tambourines on his knees, bells at his elbows, a melodeon in his hands and mouth-organ in his mouth, we gazed in wonder at the man's dexterity.

But undoubtedly the highlight of those pre-war days in our

small village was the arrival of Dick's Circus. In fact I can think of nothing which enraged me at Hitler half as much as the loss of this notable event. As a small family circus performing in the open-air and without animals, it consisted mainly of acrobatics and clowning with every member playing a part, from grandfather down to the smallest child. Under arc-lights they swung from one high bar to another, balancing on each other's heads and feet, turning somersaults and bringing roars of approval from the village folk who were not over-accustomed to entertaining spectacles. Just as important, they brought swingboats and shooting galleries and roll-a-penny stalls, and they strung lights from stall to stall and round the circus ring, powered by a dynamo and illuminating a village scene which still awaited its electricity supply. Again it brought country folk together in a warm innocence, not yet troubled by the idiocies of a world that was just around the corner. Dick's brought light to our lives and so did another little circus, Pinder's, which was slightly bigger and could stretch to a tent with a sawdust ring, a few ponies and clowns and a menagerie.

It would not have looked much to town's folk but, all things being relative, it was a spectacular show on the Market Stance at Maud. I often wondered what became of these small family circuses for they did not reappear after the war, at least not as far north as Maud. I have found no trace of the Dick family, though I believe they were miners from Fife, but I did unearth one of the Pinders in a grimy tenement in the heart of Glasgow Gorbals.

By then, Leslie Ord Pinder was in his sixties and blind. There I sat in the cheerlessness of his flat, with the eerie echoes of Glasgow's slumland outside, listening to how at least one of those small shows began. The Pinder family had been in the circus business for two hundred years, Leslie told me. They travelled around Britain and the continent bringing delight to children who no doubt thought as much of their little villages as I did of mine. Then in 1905 the big Pinder's Circus broke up in a family row, the matter went to court and the outcome was that the Big Top was divided into three smaller tops and each group went its own way. Young Leslie Pinder had gone with his parents in the show they called Captain George Pinder, His Elephants and Ponies. In the dim light I could gain only half-vision of the rotund little man with the finely shaped head as he recalled their travels around the world. Yes, he remembered our North-East villages and knew all about local legends like 'The Bonnie Lass o' Fyvie' and 'Mill o' Tifty's Annie'. But the circus travelled beyond the bounds of Scotland and it was when it reached the Far East that young Leslie saw the depressing plight of the blind, for whom there was no provision other than the right to beg. He became absorbed in their misery and spent long nights in the caravan wondering how he could help. So he set to learning Braille and the art of punching out the symbols on those sheets of brown paper which were so well known to the blind. Then, with his knowledge of the East, he busied himself in endless nights of hard work and when he emerged again he had produced a Braille edition of the Koran, the Holy Book of the Islam. Now fate, whose hand can never be ignored, played just one more of her curious cards. Leslie Pinder, still an active trapeze artist, having graduated through the ranks from programme seller in the family business, was in the prime of life when he had an accident in the ring – and lost an eye. So he became condemned to the world of half-light and shadows and more deeply involved than ever in the work of the blind.

When I met him in the bleakness of the Gorbals he was passing his days hand-punching Braille literature for any race or denomination so that they could read for themselves. He drew no financial benefit but a great deal of satisfaction from the gratitude that came to him from all over the world. Moslems knew him as Abdul Haque and wrote of him with reverence. Somewhere on the roads today there is still a Pinder's Circus for I came across their bills while motoring on the continent not so long ago.

Chapter Five

Wullie Lummies Galore

One of the excitements and minor terrors of my childhood was the sight of a formidable cart being pulled through the streets of Maud, not by a team of horses but a double row of menfolk, old and young, frail and fearsome, but all harnessed to long, strong ropes. They might be going to remove a load of dung or rubble or to help lay down the brand-new village bowling-green but whatever their purpose it was less important to us children than the fact that they were simply the Dafties.

The Buchan Combination Home in Maud was a refuge for the feeble-minded and helpless creatures of the area, sent from their various parishes, often enough because there was no relative to bear the responsibility. So they came from far and near and we would shout names at them and if one became incensed he would break away and chase us till a warder grabbed him and returned him to the yoke. But the Dafties were not all so daft. That outer crust of feebleness would often belie a keen perception from which emerged many a pure gem of philosophy.

At a higher level, one of the greatest North-East characters of all time, the inimitable Jamie Fleemin', jester to the Laird of Udny, was once being made a figure of fun by a superior gentleman in Edinburgh who, knowing full well his identity, asked Jamie who he was.

'Och, I'm the Laird of Udny's feel,' said Jamie, 'fa's feel are ye?' When he contemplated the eventual business of dying he made a special plea which became a legendary saying: 'Oh, dinna bury me like a beast.'

WULLIE LUMMIES GALORE

Maud Poorhouse was full of minor Jamie Fleemin's, oddities like Wullie Lummie (the Buchan version of William Lumsden). In the days of the shalt and gig, Wullie was walking along bare, dusty roads in the heart of Buchan when a lady-like creature stopped to offer him a lift. Wullie accepted and felt obliged to offer something in return for the ride so he asked the lady if she would like to see a photograph of himself. She said she would be delighted and adjusted her bi-focals as Wullie turned out a grubby snapshot from his inner pocket. She blinked at what she saw then, recognising a familiar building, said: 'But this is not you – this is Strichen Brewery.' 'Aye,' Wullie proudly replied, pointing to the door, 'but I'm inside washin' bottles.'

Thereafter they took him to Maud Poorhouse and yet another character was removed from the public highway. But the stories persisted. On a visit to the inmates one day, Dr McLeod was confronted by Wullie who had a complaint about the food. Producing a whole pea from the previous day's broth, he said: 'Just see foo hard that is, doctor.' Dr McLeod took the pea between his teeth and agreed that it was impossibly hard.

'Ah weel,' said Wullie, 'that's just as it came through me!'

Worthies like Wullie were a common feature of Scottish rural life and not all were locked away in institutions. They roamed the land, often hairy and unkempt, some with settled abodes and other just vagabonds picking up a night's rest wherever a farmer would give them a corner of the barn to share with the rats. Jock Pom o' New Leeds and his sister Meg were still living legends in the nineteen-thirties and so was another female figure of black terror known only as Bleedy Heids. I can still relive the paralysing fear which gripped us smaller children at Maud School when some older girls in their mischief spread word one day that Meg Pom was coming to take us away. Jock Pom was one of the hardiest nomads, often tramping along in the snow, bare-footed, up in the morning and filling himself with water brose before setting off again on his morning rounds.

Those characters were relics of the nineteenth century but I had the good fortune to have personal contact with some of them. On my visits to Mains of Whitehill, Grandpa Barron was frequently in conversation with an oddity who was in the habit of breaking into a high-pitched laugh when no-one else could see what there was to laugh about. His favourite expression was 'Nae man, nae man,' and, although his real name was Johnnie Robson, we never knew him as anything other than Johnnie Naeman. I was unaware in those childhood days that I was in the company of one of the true characters of the North-East, widely known as the Carrot King because he was such a dab hand at growing carrots. Johnnie had plots of land here and there, including one from my grandfather, on which he grew his famous vegetables. He was industrious and well-behaved and at one time the Laird of Brucklay gave him a house and a piece of land, rent-free, at Oldwhat. Johnnie was also a man of music who could fair make the melodeon dirl and he and a neighbouring farmhand, Sandy Greig, who sang bothy ballads, made a glorious team. Just think what television missed. Such focus, however, would no doubt have swept away some of the native innocence which made those people the natural, unself-conscious beings they were.

I have only secondhand accounts of some of the others, who were either past or passing when I was born but Grandpa Barron had vivid recollections of some and an old acquaint-ance, James A. F. Murray, the Poor Inspector at Maud, told me of others. Not far from my birthplace there was the Hermit of Corsegight, Robert Henry Ironside, who lived in a lonely log cabin at the top of the hill. He went about without shoes or socks, straggly hair hanging limp over his shoulders, a forerun-ner of the hippies to come. But as a young man Robert had been a schoolmaster at Mountblairy, Alvah, and had given up con-vention apparently on account of ill-health. He sought the pri-mitive ways of Nature, for which mankind regarded him as an eccentric. But he did not beg. He lived as God would provide and in pursuit of his hobby which was botany he made long journeys on foot in search of specimens. He was a man of un-doubted mental ability, scientific in a way that was well ahead of his time. Yet he chose to live in this uninhibited way, not as a gimmick like some of the oddities of a later day but because he had re-discovered the essential goodness of life.

Then there was Deaf Davie, known throughout Buchan as the Smoke Doctor, because he had a great belief in his ability to find a remedy for a reeky chimney. In his thoroughness he would plague the housewife by sitting at a fireside for hours on end, watching the progress of smoke and noting the direction of the wind. But his gift for fascinating conversation made him a tolerable and even welcome visitor. Heather Jock was a Peter-head character of untidy habits who made and sold brooms but sometimes went to Greenland on local whalers. On one occasion he entered a draper's shop where he was confronted by a large mirror. Turning to the door, he was heard to mutter: 'It's time I was oot o' this. There's eneuch o' my kind here already.' Geordie Watson wore clogs in summer and winter and became known as Cloggie, travelling the countryside with a box but never pushing trade. The goods were there if anyone wanted them but Cloggie was more interested in the latest news of local and national affairs. He was short-sighted and reading news-papers proved something of a hazard. At a farmhouse one day he was given a paper to read, with pictures of fast-going steam-ships. Cloggie was reading the thing upside down for several seconds before he exclaimed to the farmer: 'There's surely been a lot o' shipwrecks last week!'

So the names come back to memory. The Braes O' Mar, an itinerant musician who delighted old and young alike with his concertina; Gadie, an abandoned bairn found on the banks of the Gadie, at the back of Benachie, who grew up to be a ken-speckle figure, selling everything from gingerbread and candy to yellow haddies. The whole change in the pace and exposure of human activity began to iron out the creases of character and folk were soon lamenting the disappearance of the old-time worthy. But the colourful characters had not disappeared alto-gether, even if their eccentricity had diminished.

In a rather different mould, a likeable warrior called John Dickie Dempster was a regular visitor to our house at Park

Crescent. With a wife who was capable of looking after the farm at Cairnbanno, Jock spent his days scouring the countryside, buying and selling calves or ponies and picking up the news of the day. As he dumbfounded some farmer with his latest titbit, the man would feel obliged to respond with some other piece of news which was added to Jock's repertoire. He would heave his large, rugged frame across our door-step at midnight and pour out the most varied conglomeration of news and gossip, re-told in a profusion of colour and native wit, till my father swore that on days that Jock Dempster came by there was no need for *The Press and Journal*. Jock was a big, unshaven hulk of a man, smoking one quarter of his cigarette, chewing another quarter and throwing away the middle half before calling to my mother in the kitchen: 'Lord, missus, have ye ony fags? I'm clean oot.' My mother would supply the fag or more often half a packet and say: 'Ye ken, Jock Dempster, ye wid be a richt handsome chiel if ye wid shave yerself!' and the big friendly bear would grin and blush and say: 'D'ye think so, missus?' Then he would sit into the small hours telling tales of 'yon crookit oolit ò' a mannie, ye ken, John, him that sleeps wi' his brither's wife and breeds futtrats', or some lurid tale of 'yon bow-hyoched buggerick wi' the hubber an' the piner stirkies'. He could never remember the names but the description soon refreshed the listener's memory.

So Jock would arrive at a bewitching hour, perhaps with a salmon illegally extracted from the River Ythan that day, carving us a middle cut and regaling us with the news of Buchan till a calf would howl its boredom from his old black van standing outside and he would jump up saying: 'Gweed God, I've a calf to deliver tae yon weasel o' a wifie on the Hill o' Jock', and off he would go, his previous day's business not yet completed. Sometimes we cursed Jock Dempster for hours of lost sleep but he was a warm and entertaining character, an unspoiled individualist and we could not deny our affection for him.

My mother had to go for an operation and I was visiting her in an Aberdeen nursing home when there was a gentle knocking and who came sheepishly round the door but the rugged, masculine frame of Jock, shaven clean till we hardly recognised him – and carrying a bouquet of flowers. For a man who lived in a world of skittery cows and earthy talk it was the paradox to end them all. Jock sat himself down on a chair, gey ill at ease, handed my mother the beautiful bouquet, started to say something – and then burst into uncontrollable tears.

'I just canna stand tae see a body nae weel,' he sobbed as I led him out of the room and took him out of sight of my mother who had just had a major operation. I never saw Jock again. He drove off on one of his calf-hunting expeditions to the Highlands and stopped off for a cup of tea in Inverness. On the way back to the car he slumped against a lamp-post and, without time for an oath or a tear, just quietly died, a man still in his prime. Perhaps Jock and his kind were the latter-day characters, retaining that originality which is too readily smothered in our modern living. He was a native of the parish of Crimond, where they wrote the psalm tune. Nearby stands the old kirkyard of Rattray, which is now closed for burials. But they opened it up for Jock Dempster – a fitting gesture to a memorable character.

Chapter Six

Haw-Haw, Hee-Hee

Among the popular lines of conversation which still linger with me from the thirties is the one which started with 'Have ye got the Grampian yet?' Needless to say, it had nothing to do with the television station of a later date. The 'Grampian' meant the brighter world of electricity which was spreading from a scheme of that name to replace the oil lamps and Tilley mantles which remained our main source of light in my childhood. There might have been a touch of old world charm but there was precious little light from the paraffin lamps which adorned our streets in those days. They were filled and lit and extinguished by the local leerie, Sandy Kelman, whose short, quick step was a familiar sound in the gathering darkness as he marched around the village with his little ladder over his shoulder, hooking it on to the collar of the lamp-post and scaling it, up and down, up and down, till the feeble flames were flickering in their glass cases and casting down a glow which was no more than a pool at the foot of the post. It was better than nothing but what I had forgotten, until Lizzie Allan reminded me, was that Sandy's paraffin lamps were lit on alternate fortnights – the first and last quarters of the Moon. The heavenly glow was supposed to light up Maud during its more potent fortnight though the powers-that-be seemed to take little account of the clouds which would regularly obscure it and leave us to grope along with torches or lanterns. You were more than likely to plunge into the puddles which were far too common in those days of poorly-made roads.

When the Grampian finally came our way I can still recall the thrill of the new illuminations, modest though they were in retrospect. Each evening at light-up time the children would gather beneath the lofty globes to await the magic moment, then stay to gaze in wonder at the miracles of modern science. But the years of the Grampian lights and the Dicks and the Pinders were all too short. After the arguments about Edward and Mrs Simpson the whole matter seemed to be resolved with a Coronation in 1937 when they presented us with mugs adorned with the pictures of King George VI and Queen Elizabeth. Folk spoke vaguely about the Spanish Civil War but that was overtaken as a topic of conversation by Chamberlain and his visits to Hitler in Munich. To the child mind there was a certain appeal in the gathering prospect of war though, if I had known that it meant the sacrifice of the circus, the Mars and Milky Way, the Cow Candy and the black-sugar straps, not to mention the oranges, bananas and melons, I would have been persuaded to take a more pacifist stand.

Events seemed to be coming to a head when my father declared that 'as sure as God made tatties, there's gyan tae be a war'. As sure indeed. In the last days of August an evacuation officer came round to tell my father and mother that they would be expected to take two boys from Glasgow to live in our house at 2 Park Crescent if the worst came to the worst. On Saturday, 2 September, there was a great stirring in the village as militia men and Territorials looked out their uniforms and said it wouldn't be long now. Jimmy Pirie was the first to come stepping down past our house, resplendent in his uniform, pausing for a cheery farewell and declaring that he was off to the war; the train would be arriving any time now. One by one the doors were opening and the men emerging with packs on their backs, relatives fussing at their tails, as we all began to gravitate to Maud Station, where there had never been such a stir, except on Aikey Fair days. Long trains drew in from Peterhead and Fraserburgh to link up at Maud and local lads had to be summoned from the Refreshment Rooms of Lil and Lena Murison on the station platform, stuffing bottles into their hip pockets. The married men took embarrassed goodbyes of blubbering wives and bairns, for the Buchan folk are ill at ease with their emotions. But a dram helped to remove some of the inhibitions as well as blur the things that lay ahead. Single lads slubbered at their lasses and then an officer chiel from Fraserburgh, Captain Keith (who later turned up as my father-in-law!) came marching up the platform to say it was time now, time to steam away to war, to things unknown for these ploughmen and bakers, blacksmiths and vrichts, for most of whom it was an adventure to foreign parts with a purpose that was ill-defined. So they squeezed them into carriages and fastened the doors and through half-shut windows they roared their last messages to a waving, weeping crowd on the platform. The train gave a warning toot and drew slowly away, chugging up by the Den Wood and under the bridge of Old Maud Farm before turning out of our view. The folk stood there watching the smoke that hung on the distant trees and listening for the echoes which came resounding back long after it had disappeared. Then they looked at each other, said little and went home to their chappit tatties.

The void of the morning was filled in numbers at least by another train which steamed down the line from Aberdeen that afternoon. Curiosity brought out the crowds on this occasion as a horde of Glasgow children was disgorged on to the station platform in their escape from the danger of bombs in the industrial capital. Two hundred of the souls trooped off, some pale-faced and ricketty from their back-street hovels, some Irish-bred red-heads with twinkling eyes and pug noses that ran as fast as their feet. As they were marshalled into as much of an orderly column as you will achieve with industrial children, there fell upon our ears a language we had never heard before, unless we had been at the Empire Exhibition of the previous year.

'Goad, wha' a dump!' said one bubbly urchin.

'Hey Mac, whaur's ra flicks?'

We looked in dumb amazement, wholly unacquainted with the 'flicks' and such city jargon. They were marched to Victoria Hall with labels round their necks and some time after dark a car drew up outside our door and out spilled two boys, aged eleven and eight, a bit more refined than most, to be introduced as James Hyman Singer and his brother Myer from the Hillhead district of Glasgow.

Myer was a conventional little fellow but Jimmy was a strange and lonesome lad, fair-haired with prominent teeth and a filling of gold, quiet-spoken but expressing himself with long, artistic hands on which there grew at least one wart. He seemed a studious boy and if I dwell with that description it is because we could not have predicted what would come of such an extraordinary mixture. On the following week we all settled down together at Maud School, which had now doubled its roll, the Glaswegians having brought their own teachers as well as their own culture to our village scene. They were quicker and slicker in their movements having gained an agility, no doubt, from jumping on to tramcars, dashing across busy streets and running from their polis, as they called them. In Maud you heard a car at the other end of the village and had ample time to get out of its way. So the smarter city kids regarded us with some amusement, our slower country ways and speech, and they even had the audacity to mock at our dialect, apparently unaware of their own glottal sing-song. We divided into the Maud Hummlies and the Glesca Keelies, two warring factions fighting out our own battles just as our elders were preparing to do in France. Each side had its own gang hut and its leader and sometimes we would join in fierce battle, the Maud loons ramming the Keelies' hut with a full-length tree-truck which could have done mortal damage. But divine protection ensured that nothing much was to happen beyond a few black eyes and bruises.

In times of truce they would tell us of the River Clyde and the ships that sailed there, great hulking things that hooted in the fog; only months ago they had seen the *Queen Elizabeth* sail away from her launching berth, real proud they were. We heard of their flicks and fish-and-chip shops, their Rangers and Celtic, gangs and knives and bicycle chains, Barlinnie and Auchenshuggle, trams, drams and trolley-cars; and it was time to fight again, the Maud loons led by Norman Rothney, a blond warrior of the heroic type, who was strong and courageous and used his fists in the cause of justice. Boys admired him, girls adored him and as he grew up he went to fell trees in the woods and came home with bulging muscles and a fine smell of resin. By seventeen he was married and beginning to father the first of his seven children and by thirty-four he was a grandfather. Norman could take on the Glesca Keelies two or three at a time if necessary and on one occasion there was a score to settle with Jimmy Singer, our gifted evacuee. My father proposed a proper bout with boxing gloves, so the kitchen floor was cleared and battle commenced. But the first round was still young when Norman landed a punch to the mouth which was followed by a metallic ricochet around the room and an agonising yell from Jimmy that he had lost his famous gold tooth. So father marched him off to Aberdeen next day for a replacement which cost him a guinea and he swore it was the best guinea's worth he could remember. My mother fell ill and with no bad grace the Singer boys moved in with Norman and his family. But Jimmy was showing the signs of a quietly troublesome nature and on one occasion he locked himself in an upstair bedroom and Andra Forbes, the village Bobby, had to be summoned with a ladder to reach him through the window.

At Maud School, however, Jimmy Singer became the darling of the English teacher, Miss Cameron, for he was displaying a remarkable talent with words. She encouraged and guided him and was not mistaken in her declared belief that he had a future. Jimmy went back to Hyndland School, Glasgow, cut loose from a university education and began to gain a name as a poet, befriending men like Hugh MacDiarmid, Dylan Thomas, Louis MacNeice. Presenting himself now as Burns Singer, with his literary reputation on the ascendancy, he would return on occasions after the war to fawn over my mother, for whom he had a special affection, even though she had reservations about his stability and behaviour and used to express her fears to his mother.

Mrs Singer, a pale and delicate lady, could see nothing

wrong in him and dismissed the cautions but was ready to acknowledge at a later date, when Jimmy had been in a variety of trouble with the Glasgow police, that my mother had been absolutely right. He was a mixture of kindness and courtesy, drunken moods and rudeness, but all the time he was writing poetry which was widely acclaimed, as well as a memorable book about the fishing industry called *Living Silver*. One day, back in Glasgow, he arrived at the family home in 9 Ruthven Street, just off Byres Road, to find his mother hanging by the neck and he faced the appalling task of cutting her body down. Life began to straighten itself out, however, when he married Dr Marie Battle, a famous American psychiatrist, but their happiness was shortlived. He collapsed and died from a thrombosis in his early thirties with his literary potential far from fulfilled. Years later I asked Hugh MacDiarmid what might have become of him if he had lived. Would he have compared with MacDiarmid himself, regarded by many as Scotland's greatest-ever poet, surpassing Robert Burns? He pondered the question and said 'I think he might well have become a better poet than me.' So Jimmy Singer and the rest of the evacuees drifted back to Glasgow. Our Stinker Burn was no match for their mighty Clyde with its *Queen Elizabeths* and *Queen Marys*. They missed their fish and chips and their flicks and the smell of the grimy tenements and bronchial back-streets. The fresh air and country food had added pinkness to their pallor but it was poison to their souls. They had come to us when there was little need to come, when the Phoney War was dragging on, and they went back in time for the bombing they had hoped to escape.

Meanwhile the war was warming up. The tragedy of Dunkirk had echoed in our North-East corner with its call for ships of any description to sail away to the evacuation. From Fraserburgh and Peterhead they manned their tiny craft and headed off down the east coast on their way to France. In later years I was to meet a fisherman whose by-name was Daisy from St Combs and who became a legend in his lifetime for the part he played at Dunkirk. Daisy sailed his boat as near to the beaches as was possible then went ashore among the thousands of soldiers trapped with their backs to the sea. It was Britain's deadliest hour. The Germans were hot on our heels and desperate men were wading into the sea, pleading to be taken aboard some overcrowded craft. But even in dire emergency there are priorities and Daisy did not allow compassion to over-ride his main objective. So he ran up and down the beaches of Dunkirk, shouting at the pitch of his unmistakable Buchan voice: 'Is there onybody here frae St Combs, Inverallochy, Cairnbulg or the Broch (Fraserburgh)', and then, as an afterthought, 'And if there's ony room left, we'll tak folk frae Peterheid.' In the pure hell of Dunkirk, the local rivalries of the North-East fishing communities were given full expression, with the Blue Mogganers of Peterhead definitely at the end of Daisy's list! He filled his boat with room, I believe, even for a few unspecified creatures and sailed away with many a life saved. Daisy deserved his place on the roll of Dunkirk heroes.

And of course there was St Valery, high on the hill of that Normandy coast, which must for ever be a little part of Buchan and the North-East corner. For it was there that those men who drank their farewells at Maud Station and called their muted goodbyes fought their glorious battle as part of the 51st Highland Division, a losing battle that ended in death or the barbedwire captivity of the German prison camps. News filtered back that they had crossed to France with the British Expeditionary Force early in 1940 to meet the mighty German thrust that was driving towards the Channel ports. The men of the 51st went into action at Abbeville but the Hun was in command, the line of retreat was cut off and a solitary division of North-East men was left to take on the whole German Army. One of the three brigades formed an arc of protection to Le Havre but the other two were ensnared with their backs to the coast at St Valery. Back, back they went, fighting as only true Scottish blood can fight when your ammunition is no more, your casualties are colossal and those that remain are battle-weary and spent. Buchan folk don't like to give in but surrender was the only course as Rommel and his overwhelming numbers closed in. So arms went down and arms went up as they paraded away, heads hung low, to spend the next five years in German prisoner-of-war camps. It was a sorry day for Scotland with no blame attaching to the men who bore the burden. Those who defended Le Havre were successfully evacuated and became the basis of the revived 51st Division which trained for the challenge that lay ahead. By 1942 they were a vital force once more, ready to sail away that August for the start of the Desert Campaign.

Montgomery testified to their worth at Alamein when I met him in Yugoslavia after the war. Those fighting furies, bred from men who had left their fields in earlier days to draw blood as part of their land-rent, were now at war with a clearer purpose. Here was Rommel again, the man who had cut them off on the bare coast of France. Into battle they raged, guns blasting, bayonets flashing in the translucent desert light, bagpipes skirling in national fervour, with stifling sun and choking sand only minor hazards in the way of men hell-bent on winning a war. The nightmare of Alamein became the tolerable dream of Tripoli, Sicily and Italy, then it was back to Britain to prepare for the Second Front which was on everyone's lips. Off they went again that memorable D-Day of 6 June, 1944, back to the beaches of Normandy. The great drive to finish the German menace was on; and once they established themselves on French soil and took the offensive there was one object in the minds of those men from Maud and Fraserburgh and Peterhead and other North-East communities and farmsteads: St Valery. On they pushed, fighting for every field and cowshed, fortified with men and ammunition this time – and the memory of 1940. The Germans stuck grimly to their occupation of France but mile by mile they were blasted out of position till that precious moment arrived. Led by the men who had fought for their lives on that same coast, the Highland Division thundered into St Valery, back to settle a small account, albeit four years later. But the war had still to be won and they played a notable part in the rest of the drive through Europe and were the last infantry of the British Second Army to be in operation against the enemy. What a fitting operation it was. Near Bremerhaven they brought about the surrender of the much-admired 15th Panzer Grenadiers, their old combatants in North Africa. The account had finally been closed. Half-an-hour later, the Armistice terms were signed on Luneberg Heath.

Meanwhile Lord Haw-Haw (an Irishman called William Joyce who was working for German propaganda radio) was drawling out his regular bulletins in an attempt to undermine British morale. 'Gairmany calling, Gairmany calling' he used to begin, as we fiddled with the wireless knobs to make sure that we didn't miss his broadcasts. Almost invariably he was capable of shattering us with items of completely authentic news. 'The town clock at Forres stopped at one minute to midnight last night' was the kind of intelligence he was able to impart. 'Hitler will be in Scotland in time to perform the opening ceremony of the new bridge over the Ythan at Ellon'. Someone was obviously keeping him well informed and almost inevitably the word spread around that we had a spy in our midst. Everyone knew his name and he had a moustache and folk said it would just be like him to consort with the Nazis. Neighbours downstairs swore that they heard a radio transmitter in the room above but nothing was ever established and the man was probably completely innocent.

Churchill had made his famous speech about fighting them on the beaches and in the streets and I can still remember the confidence his voice instilled in the child. He may have been a man of many faults but forever after that he held the gratitude of children who felt that as long as he stood between them and Hitler no great harm would come. The way he spat out the word 'Nazi' left no doubt about his feelings, which were very much the same as my own child-like sentiments since the day I suffered from German measles. In addition to the strength of Churchill we were also blessed with the courage and fortification of the Local Defence Volunteers, later known as the Home Guard and the model from which the television people eventually gave us 'Dad's Army'.

Since my father had failed his medical for the forces he was a ripe candidate for the L.D.V. He was stout and suffered from a slight heart condition so they made him a captain. Death and insanity were the only possible grounds for exemption (not that you would always have noticed!), leaving a wide range of conditions for the ranks of the L.D.V. As my father rasped out his orders, a motley collection of mis-shapes who had come straight from field or work-bench jumped as near to attention as could be expected and off they would march in a zany column, with the left-rights about equally balanced by the right-lefts. There were the long and thin, the short and fat, the ploughman and the postman, the vricht and the grocer. But within such military inadequacy there was at least ample room for promotion. You could become a colonel with carbuncles or a lance-corporal with gout. They marched off on schemes, route marches and mock battles with camouflaged coverings that made them look like cows peering through a hedge. They would duck down behind ditches, reappear in a frenzy of battle activity and argue among themselves as to who was dead and who was not. Sometimes we boys would hide behind a dyke and call out 'L.D.V. – Look, Dook and Vanish!' and there was a stramash till we were hunted out like German snipers and delivered of a hefty kick on the backside. They built a pill-box by the village crossroads, at the top of the Bobby's Brae, with little holes through which they intended to shoot every German who came in sight. We were totally unfair to the L.D.V. of course, showing a cynicism which seems to thrive in Scotland, but I had an uncanny feeling that if the German invaders got as far as Maud they were unlikely to fail at the final hurdle of our fireside soldiers. Mercifully it was never put to the test and they remain but a memory, one of the many diversions which made the war years tolerable and sometimes even amusing. They had started with nothing but a forage cap and a khaki armband but soon they were fully dressed soldiers and, among my many souvenirs, I keep intact to this day my father's battledress with his three pips of a captain, a piece of moth-eaten nostalgia for a phase of history when the real and the unreal were never so closely wedded.

One of the attractions of the war to a country child was the unaccustomed bustle it created in places where visitors were about as scarce as hen's teeth. Great battalions of soldiers came driving in with heavy lorries and bren-gun carriers, and aerodromes sprang up at places like Longside and Crimond where sheep had grazed before, since we were the nearest point in Britain to Norway and the whole of northern Europe. The Russian convoys passed along our coast before heading out towards the Baltic and we would rush to the coast to watch this mysterious movement of ships, realising that we lived in stirring times. In Maud they commandeered Kerr's Hall and Victoria Hall, where they had held grand balls before the war and visiting repertory companies of professional actors used to present plays like *Alf's Button*. Now a thousand soldiers came to billet themselves in the village and at Brucklay Castle, two miles up the road – men of the King's Own Scottish Borderers who had come to prepare for the Second Front. What mattered more to me was that they had a pipe band. I had always wanted to play the pipes, ever since the days when the Gordon Highlanders had come on their pre-war recruiting drives, enlisting many a whisky-laden farm servant who had come to Maud with the innocent intention of taking a fee from a farmer and found himself next day with the arles of His Majesty and a posting to Gibraltar. I made myself known to Jock Gray from Kelso, who fair could make the pigskin skirl (he later moved to the Royal Scots Greys and formed the band which was to gain fame with *Amazing Grace*). Jock took me in hand in his spare time and taught me to play the chanter, which is the preliminary of the full-scale business of playing the pipes. You learn the fingering on the chanter, which is just a glorified penny-whistle with a reed giving out a mellow sound. Through the winter months of 1942–43 I deaved the neighbourhood with practice till I had a repertoire of three tunes, *Highland Laddie*, *The 79th Farewell to Gibraltar* and *The Green Hills of Tyrol*, before Andy Stewart gave it words and called it *The Scottish Soldier*. Everywhere the Kosbies went I was sure to go, striding along on route marches or church parades till the commanding officer did not have the heart to send me away. All the time I was helping in the kirk canteen, cajoling my mother to house the wives who came to visit their husbands and generally acting as mascot to the battalion.

On a glorious day in 1943 we had our one and only visit from Royalty, who would have little cause to pass our way at any other time. The KOSB had as their colonel-in-chief the Duchess of Gloucester, who arrived in splendour and inspected the children of Maud School in the village Pleasure Park before visiting her battalion at Brucklay. We followed her to the castle to share in the massive military spectacle, the like of which we had never seen in Buchan. The pipes and drums combined with the military band to give the most glorious musical performance and as I ran home late for my tea I can still remember pausing in the quiet of an April evening as the sound of the silver band came echoing through the Brucklay trees. The tune was Lehar's *Gold and Silver* and if there are moments in life which have the pureness of heaven on earth, which you try to fix in your consciousness because they will not come again, then this was one for me. I had my comfortable structure of life, easy and familiar and enriched for the moment at least by real, live soldiers and a Royal visitor and thrilling music. What more could a schoolboy want to fulfil his dreams of happiness?

Two weeks later the KOSB played for us again, this time in the village square, a full muster of bandsmen beating out the majesty of Retreat. Alas, it was to be the retreat from our village scene as well, a final tribute to folk who had opened their homes and their hearts to bring a touch of comfort to those Borderers, country folk like ourselves from the farms and mill towns at the other end of Scotland, who were now marching away to continue their D-Day training at Hayton Camp, Aberdeen. Trucks and bren-gun carriers led the way and, as the men stepped off on their twenty-eight mile march, a whole village turned out, every man, woman and child, to see them on their way. The bottom was about to fall out of my world. Once again I filed alongside the soldiers, the rich smell of their khaki tunics, their blanco and their boots, and marched till they were at Auchnagatt and the waves and cheers of the Maud folk had faded into the past. They fell out for a rest and when they formed up again Jock Gray put a hand on my shoulder and told me it was time to go home now or my mother would be worrying; big, friendly Jock, my wartime hero who epitomised the warmth and kindliness of Border folk. Yes, they would come back to see us and I would visit them in their part of Scotland when the war was over. So they formed up and, with a left and a right, they marched out of my life, these young soldiers, some of them never to come home from the battlefields of Europe. I stood there incapable of words, reminding myself that brave soldiers do not cry. I watched and waved, fighting back the lump in my throat, and they turned and waved back and when they were only a hazy mass on a distant horizon the bung dropped out and the tears came flooding to blur the final vision. I turned and ran back to the village and the wind dried the tears, leaving stains which told their own story.

Long after the war was over and they were back in their beloved Borders as veterans of a nightmare war that had now slipped away, they invited their Maud mascot as a guest at their reunion dinner in the Crown Hotel in Hawick. I was not prepared for a speech because that had not been the intention. But the chairman asked if I would like to say a few words and I felt it in my heart to do so. It was a night of beer and bonhomie when speeches were regarded as something of an intrusion upon the revelry of the moment. But as I rose to survey the ranks of familiar faces, which time had altered with lines and specks of grey, there was a sudden shuffle of attention for the boy from Maud who had grown to a man with less hair than most of themselves. Straight out of the memory and the heart I took them back to those days in Maud, when they were in their twenties and early thirties, and gave them a sight of themselves through the eyes of a child. I could point to men I had not seen for thirty years and give them names and memories of their younger days which apparently touched them deeply and I could equally remember the ones who were gone. Suddenly I realised that the beer glasses were standing untouched on the tables and the men who were now in their fifties and sixties were silently engrossed in a bygone age.

Speech-making has never been a strength of mine but what I had to say was at least plain and sincere and I could see clearly that there were tears on many a cheek. So I finished abruptly and sat down and there was a pause of several seconds. Then those veterans of the Second World War, my young heroes of 1942, burst into a deafening applause and rose to their feet as a solid body to give the loon from Maud a standing ovation. It was a highly-charged moment and needless to say we delved deeper into the nostalgia, as well as the whisky bottles, before the night was out! Only the presence of Jock Gray could have made it better, but Jock was no longer with us.

By the time these men had marched out of my life in 1943 I had my own bagpipes and could play them, thanks to Jock, and when the war was nearly over and the L.D.V. (by then the Home Guard) decided that, in the absence of any Germans, it could now safely disband, I stepped out with another boy piper, Willie Stables, to lead them in their farewell parade.

Long before then, however, the routine of wartime had become as familiar as the peace-time days of the thirties. Schooldays were joyously broken with air-raid drill, when Donald Murray, the headmaster, would blow a loud whistle and we would drop pencils and dash home, run once round the table and back to school. Sometimes the air-raids were for real as German bombers came trundling over Buchan, seeking out the Fraserburgh Toolworks or merely shedding their bombs as British fighters made chase to intercept. Their explosions blew craters in many a nearby field and on one occasion a plane of our own came crashing down in a field at Cairndale and we all ran up after school to see the burning shell. Farm children were allocated a village house as a refuge during air-raids and I was paired with Jimmy Allan from Bulwark, a droll lad with a long, solemn face but a quick mother-wit when he cared to speak. In return for the cups of tea during air-raids, he appeared at my mother's doorstep one Christmas morning with a turkey. Never a word was spoken as he held out the bulging bird. My mother, taken aback by the generosity, said: 'Oh Jimmy, this is surely nae for me?' Whereupon he surveyed her disdainfully and replied: 'Fa the hell ither?' Buchan drollness at its best.

At school we learned our three Rs, passing up the line from Miss Catto's infant class to Miss Duncan and Mrs Gregor, who had been coaxed out of retirement. The arrival of an auburn-haired lady called Miss Morrison was a fortuitous coincidence with the stirring of interest in the fair sex. I can still remember her breezy walk, the toss of her head and the silk-stockinged legs upon which the boy could play out his first eager fantasies. Miss Auchinachie, with a bun in her hair, came to teach us music and a continental lady called Miss Feltges put us through dancing routines and thought that I was sufficiently well blessed with rhythm that I should demonstrate with Margaret Cassie, whose body movement was exquisite.

At home we listened to the wireless with its news bulletins brought by announcers who had to identify themselves for authenticity, in contrast to the earlier anonymity. So they began: 'Here is the news, read by Frank Phillips . . . or Joseph McLeod ... Alvar Liddell ... Bruce Belfrage....' We listened to Reginald Foort at the BBC theatre organ, to *Band Wagon*, with Stinker Murdoch and Arthur Askey, as well as to *Happidrome*, with Mr Ramsbottom, Mr Lovejoy and Enoch singing:

> We three
> in harmony
> Working for the BBC
> Ramsbottom and Enoch and me . . .

And the talk of war wore on as the dominant theme of living, with every household pinning a map on the wall and moving little pointers which kept us up-to-date on the advances and retreats of the German and Allied forces. Arguments raged about who was going to win and how long it would last but I remember the general consensus was that it would run for all of ten years. 'It'll get waur afore it's better,' folk said with gloom in their voices. Well, it did get waur, as they forecast, but it did come to an end in six years instead of ten. And when the great upheaval ended and the crowds were thronging London to celebrate Victory in Europe, we had our own VE Night on the site of a burned-out garage, heaping old wood and tyres into a pile and enflaming it with paraffin till a glorious bonfire lit up the night sky of Tuesday, 8 May, 1945, and we celebrated the final destruction of Adolf Hitler. In no time at all the northern lights of the Grampian supply went up again and folk began to see a world they scarcely recognised. That bonfire glow which symbolised the end of Hitler was viewed with pensive gloom by hundreds of German soldiers, captured by the troops who went off to the D-Day invasion of France and sent back as prisoners-of-war to camps around our Buchan district. They worked on farms and we came to know them and to marvel at the fact that they were recognisable human beings, some just youngsters who had been conscripted into the Hitler Youth and sent off to combat the D-Day invasion when the fluff was scarcely off their chins.

Werner Hoffman had just started as a student at Heidelberg University when he was spirited off to battle, en route to captivity at Stuartfield. He was just one of several young lads – 'They're a' somebody's bairn' as my mother used to say – who were welcomed to our house for tea on Sundays. Not all were disillusioned with their Führer at that stage but we kept clear of the topic and treated them with courtesy and hospitality.

The British Government kept its prisoners till 1948, when we shook hands and wished them a better future. In the years between, I have motored a good deal across the continent and have never failed to call on Werner Hoffman when passing through the Heidelberg district, where he is a prosperous business-man with a charming family. He has entertained me to tea on Sundays, returning the compliment of my mother's table at 2 Park Crescent, Maud, and we have raised a glass of schnapps, agreed about the madness and futility of war and toasted the day when mankind will learn to live in peace.

Chapter Seven

In Memory

Now that the war was over and the dust was settling, the kirk bells rang out one memorable Sunday, peeling from the Low Village right up through the quiet streets of Maud, beckoning old and young to gather round in memory of the men who had fallen. And in our quiet way we answered the call, near every walking soul of us, down to the granite slab that stood in the corner by the kirk. Its front was already well covered with the names of our village men who came to grief in what they called The Great War of 1914–18. There were not so many names this time for the total massacre was not so vast but the field of Flanders had broadened to take in the sands of the desert and the angry fathoms of the Atlantic. And we remembered. Sonny Barrie, who gave us lifts on the step of his bike that last leave before he rode away to his death; Patty Gordon, a studious boy who had been scarce away from Maud School when he was drowning at Narvik; Bertie Kelman who went down in the last weeks; Johnny Wallace, whose daughter Jean was left fatherless in my class, as we tried in our own awkward way to be kind. And the others.

We were a little village, just one of thousands whose dead were no more dead than the rest, but no less either, so we somehow embodied the whole tragedy of the situation, the price that was paid in simple human lives for the antics of a madman. A Union Jack covered the memorial as we bowed our heads and heard the minister say his say about our dear ones who had gone away without thought of self and had fought and died for the love of their country. You pondered the man's

66

words and considered whether they had really gone with such patriotic purpose or whether it was more in the heat and spirit and compulsion of the moment, with the optimism which keeps most of us going in this bewildering world of ours.

So we sang a hymn and there was a scurrying as Mrs Chrissie Heddle stepped forward to pull the flag from the stone. She must have had her own memories for it was her husband, George Heddle, the local road surveyor, who mustered a company of our local county council roadmen to sail as a unit of the Royal Engineers for some secret destination abroad. Their ship, an old Egyptian tub called the *Mohammed-Ali-el-Kabir*, was somewhere in the dark Atlantic when it was torpedoed by a German U-boat which had waited until the escorting vessel was round the other side before piercing the troopship with a deadly weapon. Among the men who flailed about in dark and stormy seas was my uncle, John Argo, whose predicament was made worse when they threw down liferafts on top of the help-less soldiers and broke his back. Some were drowned and others maimed and the memory of it bore heavily on their leader who survived the war but died soon after.

We bowed our heads in prayer and I was back again in the infant class of pre-war days when we lowered our eyes for an Armistice Day that was vague and distant in its image. This time we knew more about the realities, about the men who had fought in the dubs and kyirn of the battlefield till they sweated the crimson sweat of death, a sweat that does not dry away but only hardens to a crust.

And there as they lay, with the blast of gunfire in their ears, the smell of cordite in their nostrils, I wondered if these men, who had thought little of danger when they rode off that September day and who were ill at ease with kirks and religion, came face to face with the truth of their plight, if they drew a lung-racking breath to utter from parched lips a prayer that was maybe their first and surely their last. And as the noise and stench of battle began to fade I knew that their thoughts would be with fadder and bridder in the parks of Buchan, pu'in' neeps in the wind and carting them to the neepshed with a curse for the bite of the blast or the sweirty of the horse. Or perhaps with midder washing eggs in the kitchen, little knowing that the son who tugged at her breasts those years ago lay dying in the helplessness of some foreign field.

Now the sotter of it all tore at the child heart as fadder and midder and bridder were seated in the glum silence of the next-of-kin, fighting back the tears that are seldom shed in Buchan. As the minister finished, a shrill wind blew up and darkness came early from Bulwark. Folk looked around and nodded one to the other in the silence which says so much in rural Scotland. So we went up the village that day, home to our little homes, leaving the cold grey granite with its poppies and flowers and black-printed names that are aye ready to tell a story to those who will pause and wonder.

Chapter Eight

From Whitehill to the White House

At the country school of Whitehill my great-grandfather, Gavin Greig, had his share of natural talent but never one of such worldly promise as little Bertie Forbes, the baggy-breeked son of Robbie Forbes, the local tailor whose shop also dispensed the district supply of porter and ale. Out of poor and humble circumstances here was a rare talent which Gavin Greig set about fostering with tuition, books and encouragement. When the time came for Bertie to leave school, he told Maister Greig that he wanted to write. But the centres of journalism were far from Whitehill and the best that could be found for him was a job as a printer's devil on the *Peterhead Sentinel*, under the guidance of Dauvit Scott. He spent three years of typesetting there before joining the Dundee *Courier* as a reporter. When the Boer War advertised South Africa he landed in Johannesburg in time to team up with Edgar Wallace, the thriller writer, who was about to establish the *Rand Daily Mail*. At twenty-three he was the journalistic prodigy of the Veldt, worming out exclusives from important gold men, having eavesdropped on their conversations as he caddied on the golf courses of Johannesburg. Edgar Wallace allowed the young Forbes to write the Wallace column under the master's name, such was his regard for the Scots lad. He had already gone far since he walked from Whitehill School but his interest in the financial world of stocks and shares drew him inevitably to New York.

A growing reputation in South Africa, however, counted for nothing in America where it was fairly bluntly conveyed to him that the big financial dailies had little use for a Scottish country bumpkin who hardly knew Wall Street from Broadway. But the shrewd little Bertie, bumpkin or not, had the last word when he cunningly offered to work for nothing. Well, gee, there wasn't much to lose with a guy who worked for nothing and the New York *Journal of Commerce* unbent. After a week's work they made him a fifteen-dollar-a-week junior at the age of twenty-four and when Edgar Wallace offered him the London correspondent's post of the *Rand Daily Mail* six months later he had already made such an impression that the *Journal* gave him his choice of job. In his rapid promotion, he picked an important desk in the financial department and soon became editor. Bertie still remembered that the value of a dollar, like the bawbee he so seldom had to spare at Whitehill, depended on how it was spent.

In 1905, for example, he gave up his New York lodgings and moved into the old Waldorf Astoria, the meeting place of America's mighty men. While it cost him more than he was earning, it brought him an unrivalled amount of what the newspaper world calls 'contacts'. At thirty-two he was well settled in double anonymity as financial editor for the *Journal of Commerce* and editorial writer for the *Commercial and Financial Chronicle*. At that time the New York *American* was looking for a business editor and narrowed its choice to two men – both of whom turned out to be B.C. Forbes.

From there he began to make a deep impression on the business world of America, which had been accustomed to a form of journalism as innocuous as the business world wanted it to be. The dynamic Forbes demanded the right to express his personal view in the *American*, translating economics into the sort of copy which could have been understood by his old father at Whitehill. He shattered smugness, stirred the conscience of the moguls and became known as the humanizer of American business. He was now in such a position of knowledge and power that the next step seemed inevitable. Why not start his own business journal? So in 1917 the first issue of *Forbes Magazine* appeared on the stalls with the opening line: 'Business was originated to produce happiness, not pile up millions. Are we in danger of forgetting this?' It took the simple logic of a baggy-breeked boy from the backwoods of Scotland to drive home the lesson to the mighty men of America. In the same issue he flayed George Jay Gould, scion of Jay Gould's $80 million rail-road empire, headlining him as 'A highly-placed misfit' and attributing the dissipation of the Gould system to George's 'narrowness of vision, unreasoning jealousy, distrust of both subordinates and rivals'. At the same time he offered a thousand dollars for the best essay on 'Who is the best Employer in America?' The magazine was not an immediate financial success and there were many Fridays when Bertie did not know where the wages were coming from. But he kept going with the determination which made Gavin Greig so sure that he had a winner in the class. The romantic stories continued, as did the windmill tilting in the classic Don Quixotic pattern. The boldest was the serialised searing of Henry Ford in 1927 ('Slave-driving in Ford Factories' etc). When some readers protested he wrote an editorial entitled 'Please cancel your subscriptions'. He then underlined the independent attitude with a rataplan of critical editorials about the R.J. Reynolds Tobacco Company, a crusade which lost him Camel advertising but left his self-respect intact.

Between issues he managed to write eleven books, to found the Investors' League in America and eventually to receive the recognition of an honorary degree from the University of Southern California and the Freedom Foundation Award 'for outstanding achievement in bringing about the better understanding of the American way of life'.

With his plush offices in New York's Fifth Avenue, Bertie Forbes had come a long way. But with the making of millions he never forgot the place where he began. Every two years there was a stirring of excitement in the parish when a chauffeur-driven Rolls Royce appeared over the horizon as Bertie and his entourage came home to visit old friends, having collected his surviving brothers and sisters on the way to share a few days at the scene of their youth. Bertie's Picnic became a major event, from the days of my mother's childhood, when they all piled into horse-drawn carts and journeyed to the beach at New Aberdour, where the sea smells better than anywhere else. By the time of my own acquaintance in the mid-thirties they were held in fields adjoining Gavin Greig's old school, where he had received all his formal education. There were races for children and adults alike, prizes and gifts for all and a word of encouragement from the man himself. He had a special affection for the Greig descendants and in the evenings of his visit he would entertain my parents and grandparents and other relatives to dinner at the Cruden Bay Hotel, which was the Gleneagles of the North-East in those days, served by a permanent way which its railway owners had laid from Ellon, as a tangent of the Buchan line. Sometimes I was allowed to join the party and to listen to the talk of a man who was on first-name terms with men like John D. Rockefeller and Frank Woolworth and who played Saturday night card games with George Gershwin's mother when the great American composer was just a lad about the house.

Bertie Forbes would encourage my interest in newspapers by telling me stories of his dealings with William Randolph Hearst, the most powerful newspaper owner in the world; of how Hearst had offered him a blank cheque to write for his empire and how he had assessed his own worth at a ridiculously high figure which was accepted without question. He was the first person we ever knew with a cine-camera and on the following visit he would show films of Hillie or Waulkie or the Miller running races and receiving their prizes and then, with a mischief which showed that he had not forgotten the value of a bawbee, he would reverse the reel and we saw the same people handing back their prize-money and running backwards like a lot of lunatics from a Keystone Cops adventure.

Since I was a direct descendant of his own boyhood hero, who had encouraged his career in journalism, he was by way of repaying a debt through an awe-struck lad who was only too glad to sit with his mouth open and savour that first rub with greatness. The name of Gavin Greig had hovered as an inspi-

Gavin Greig, my great-grandfather, who became Scotland's greatest-ever collector of folk songs.

The Marchioness of Aberdeen opens a fete at Brucklay Castle, Maud, in 1934. I am in my mother's arms, fifth from the left.

Coronation Day, 1937.
In fancy dress parade at
Maud, my rajah outfit
takes second place to the
red, white and blue of
Sandy Duncan, now the
local butcher.

opposite
As a young reporter
(centre) on the *Turriff
Advertiser*, with the
proprietors, W. D. Peters
and his son Bob.

Fun at marquee dance
after the 'wash-out'
Turriff Show of 1949 –
with my editor, Donald
Noble, brother of Sir
Fraser Noble, Principal
of Aberdeen University.

Bertie Forbes, the New
York millionaire, with
my parents.

Aikey Fair, Scotland's only continental Sunday, as it can still be seen every July, on a lonely hillside near Maud.

A jolly night at the fabulous Forbes party, with the Vice President of the United States, Senator Hubert Humphrey, Agnes Baird and Gertrude Weiner.

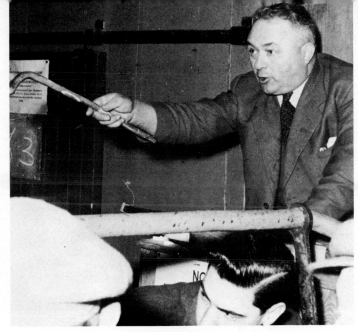

My father as thousands remember him, selling cattle at
Maud Mart.

Honeyneuk Farm, Maud, which my father bought in 1952.

My farewell night at Aberdeen Journals, February 1960.

In the hot seat at Albion Street, Glasgow, as Chief Sub-Editor of *Scottish Sunday Express*.

The KOSB reunion in Hawick, with soldiers I had known in Maud in 1942–3.

With Bing Crosby and his two sons at Turnberry Hotel.

A meeting with Maud's most illustrious native, Lesley Storm, the world-famous playwright and novelist.

Maud, with part of Honeyneuk Farm in background.

ration for as long as I could remember and now his pupil was adding a more immediate stimulus to the ambition which would lead me, surely, towards a writing career.

Bertie endowed his old school and the parish church at nearby New Deer. There are annual prizes of Bibles for children's attendance at the church, an encouragement in the ways of worship which were such an important part of his childhood at Whitehill. On his seventieth birthday he presented a baptismal font and was there at its dedication. It would be hard to forget the scene as he stood by the font, a powerful man of high places, and watched with tears on his cheeks as a humble child of his native parish was anointed with water from the same burn as his own christening water.

Who would know? Perhaps another lad o' pairts was on the way, for Bertie did not believe that the days of opportunity were over. His visits were always in the summer and he came again two years later. A further two years should have elapsed before his next visit but as December approached, word got round that Bertie Forbes was coming at Christmas, the first time he had ever made such a return to the old corner. No one knew why he came, only that he played Father Christmas and spoke to the children of the thrift and honesty and hard work that were ingrained in his Scottish character and which would enable them to lead happy, contented lives. Older men sensed that there was a longing in his eyes, that last embracing look at things which are of the beginning. Somehow the gloss of the big-time American with a life-long experience of Wall Street, the White House and the Waldorf Astoria peeled away and he became a child again, back at the Cunnyknowe where he was born, polishing boots for the local gentry, gathering peats and heading off to school and the strict discipline of Maister Greig.

Then his chauffeur drew up at our door at Maud, where he made his last call, and Bertie stepped into the limousine with his ever-faithful secretary, Gertrude Weiner, who had been with him since the very early days of *Forbes Magazine*; he bade us all a very thoughtful goodbye and rode away over the hill by Old Maud, back to his adopted world of Manhattan. His instinct for life and death was as sure as his instinct for business because, just as he must have calculated himself, the daylight was running out. A few months later they found him slumped at his desk, having died in the way he had lived – with a pen in his hand. The financial empire is now run by one of his five sons, Malcolm, who was tipped as a future President of the United States during the fifties, when he rose to be the bright young hope of the Republican Party at roughly the same time as John F. Kennedy was blossoming for the Democrats. But it was the Irishman who strode on to become President while the Scot was turning to follow in his father's footsteps.

Malcolm Forbes has taken his father's foundations and extended them from the field of journalism into business ventures and land ownership of such a scale that Bertie Forbes could not have dreamed about. He has emerged as one of the richest and most extraordinary of American business men, world-famous as a hot-air balloonist and the owner of the Governor's Palace in Morocco, a massive chateau in France, Battersea House in London and a whole island in the Pacific, not to mention his own DC9 airplane and the biggest yacht in New York Harbour.

Bertie had invited my father and mother to the various anniversary gatherings of *Forbes Magazine*, including the thirtieth celebration, which was to act as a springboard for the Presidential candidacy of Thomas Dewey. However, a journey to New York seemed out of the question for folk from Maud in those days. But I vowed to myself that, at some time in the future, at least one member of the family would make a belated response to the invitation from the man who had finally inspired me on the road to journalism. The occasion lay many years ahead – but I had a good idea who that person would be!

Chapter Nine

C'mon The Dons!

It was right in the heart of the Second World War that I savoured the true essence of Aberdeen when, on the basis of an I.Q. test, I was despatched for the purpose of developing an intelligence which was allegedly worth developing, though subsequent events were to cast some doubt on the theory. The choice was a straightforward one between Aberdeen Grammar, Lord Byron's old school, and Robert Gordon's College. The Grammar had the upper-crust image while Gordon's, with its bursaries and Scatterty Scholarships, was said to find a better social balance, mixing clever laddies from working-class city homes with the affluence of west-end fish and granite and the plain dyst of country loons.

So I strolled through the vaulted gateway of Robert Gordon's in Schoolhill at a time when Hitler was dropping his bombs on the major cities, into a world of black gowns and musty corridors, blue blazers and grey flannel pants, rugby, science and swimming, which was producing assorted heroes with names like Frank Thomson (later to become a controversial entrepreneur in the Highlands), I.D. Ewen, St Clair Taylor and Johnny Rose and had yet to produce an Olympic champion by the name of Ian Black. A jovial chap called John Smith used to hold court in the playground with all the aᴗsurance which later turned him into Lord Kirkhill; and among other contemporaries with whom I made my debut as an amateur actor was a solemn-faced boy from the Hilton district called Buff Hardie, later to gain fame as part of the *Scotland the What?* phenomenon.

Life at Gordon's was centred on a main building which had changed little since the butcher Cumberland billeted his men there on the march north for the Battle of Culloden and again on his way home, when he plundered and raped the city and citizens of Aberdeen in a most despicable manner. Robert Gordon had been a local merchant who made his fortune while trading in Danzig and who set up a 'hospital', which was a school for the poor boys of his native city, in 1732. The boys were known as Sillerton Loons. The centuries had turned the hospital into a great centre of learning, incorporating not only a day school but a technical college, art college and schools of architecture and navigation – and a boys' boarding-house which was called Sillerton House. So once again we were back with the original name of Sillerton Loons, of whom I became one, having been sent there after a spell in lodgings with Miss Stott in Elm Place, during which I had displayed a rare talent for putting football before fractions, pictures well ahead of Pythagoras. Snack bars and smokey cinemas, forbidden Wood-bines and billiard salons (enriched by the coffee aroma from Collie's shop in Union Street) were much in vogue in the forties when the News Cinema in Diamond Street would provide, with commendable speed, a Monday showing of the Aberdeen football team's feats of the previous Saturday. Even with its immediacy, television can provide nothing of the atmosphere of those large-scale, ground-level projections.

The war was drawing to a close and big names of the thirties were returning to grace the turf of Pittodrie Park, which had been the home of Aberdeen F.C. since its inception in 1903. As I recall in another book, 'The Dons,' my wartime hero of the football field had been Johnny Pattillo, a bow-legged centre-forward with middle parting and lethal shot, but now he was being joined by players like George Hamilton and Archie Baird, two of the memorable thoroughbreds of football who had been employing their talents in more hostile pursuits these last six years.

Winston Churchill came driving up Union Street in an open car to celebrate victory over the Hun and to receive the

Freedom of the City in the same month as the Dons carried off
their very first honour at national level, the Scottish League
Cup of 1946. It was a reflection of the farcical state of Scottish
football that it had taken all that time for a single reward to get
so far away from the Glasgow stranglehold of Rangers and
Celtic. During the forty-three year period from 1904 till 1947
the Scottish League Championship was won once by Mother-
well and on every other occasion by either Rangers or Celtic,
with their large hordes of supporters who came to regard domi-
nance as their birthright. How the game survived that appalling monopoly is more than I shall ever understand. Yet those
old men who remembered the very beginnings of Pittodrie
football would positively glow with happy recollection, if not of
silverware success at least of great personalities who had graced
the Merkland Road turf through close on half a century. There
were names like Willie Lennie, Aberdeen's first Scottish inter-
nationalist, Donald Colman and Jock Hume, a famous fullback
partnership to be followed by an equally effective pair in Jock
Hutton and Matt Forsyth. There was that elegant member of
the Wembley Wizards team, Alec Jackson, and a bouncy little
Aberdonian by the name of Benny Yorston, regarded by many
as the greatest Dons player of them all.

Brilliance continued through the thirties with men like the
stylish Willie Mills and here we were in the forties, now coping
with the turmoil and confusion of the world's most devastating
war. From a football point of view the consolation for North-
East people was that it brought some big names from the south
to play at Pittodrie. In the great movement of armed forces, an
airman billeted locally turned out to be Stanley Mortensen,
later to become one half of a legendary partnership with Stanley
Matthews for both Blackpool and England. During two
seasons Mortensen was a guest player with Aberdeen, as was
the habit of the time, scoring memorable goals and winning a
host of friends in the North-East.

It was around that time that my mother and I were travelling
to Aberdeen on the Buchan train one day in the company of
Hector Mavor, the village joiner, who asked if I had ever been

to Pittodrie. Youthful eyes glowed with interest for I knew the names and reputations though I had never been inside a football ground in my life. The soccer horizons had not extended beyond the Pleasure Park at Maud where some gory battles were fought out under the banner of the Buchan League. At least our village had contributed one player to the ranks of Aberdeen Football Club – goalkeeper Jimmy Henry, whose father owned the Station Hotel – but now Hector Mavor was offering to take me on my very first visit to Pittodrie while my mother went shopping, and she didn't have the heart to say no. So that afternoon in 1942 I set my disbelieving eyes on Pittodrie Park for the first time, to watch an Army select team playing Aberdeen.

But now in 1946, when a trophy had been won at long last, Aberdeen were poised to become an even greater force in Scottish football. Within a year they had done it again, this time going one better to win the more prestigious Scottish Cup. Only once before had they even reached the final of the national trophy. That was in 1937, when they were beaten by Celtic in a match which set an all-time crowd record of 146,433 for a club encounter in the British Isles. The disappointment of that result had been quickly followed by a tour of South Africa which brought the tragedy of Jackie Beynon, Aberdeen's popular outside right who was rushed to hospital in Johannesburg with an appendicitis – and died of peritonitis. The bitter memory of 1937 still lived with men like Willie Cooper, George Johnstone and Frank Dunlop, who survived to play again ten years later as Aberdeen embarked on another Scottish Cup competition. There was high excitement at Pittodrie with the first-round victory over Partick Thistle, gained by a last-minute goal from the veteran Willie Cooper, a loyal servant who was by then in his twentieth season with the Dons.

Come April of 1947 and we were delving into drawers to unearth any garment with red in it, for Aberdeen had reached the Scottish Cup final at Hampden Park, Glasgow, and the wartime austerity of clothing coupons was still with us. So my mother converted her only red jumper into a tammy with a tassle on top and off I went, an eager fifteen-year-old, to my first adventure as a Dons' supporter. Alas, as we boarded the special trains at the Joint Station that Saturday morning we knew that the Aberdeen team would be without the man who had made it all possible. Willie Cooper had been injured in the semi-final of the previous week. This was Willie's last chance to win any kind of medal and fate had done him an injustice. The opposition that day was Hibernian and after a disastrous start, in which they lost a silly goal in the first minute, Aberdeen came storming back to win by 2–1, little Stan Williams scoring one of the cheekiest of all goals.

As captain Frank Dunlop held the Cup aloft, Aberdonians in the vast crowd began to chant 'We want Cooper'. Willie was coaxed from his seat in the shadows to receive the acclaim of a grateful public. There he stood, a shy man near to tears, holding the Scottish Cup and absorbing a precious moment in football history. Those of us on the terracing with lumps in our throats had not yet formulated the thought. For sure, there had been a colourful and illustrious past at Pittodrie, with names to inspire an impassioned memory. But what we had just witnessed that April day in 1947 was the final arrival of Aberdeen on the scene of Scottish football.

Chapter Ten

The Betty Hadden Mystery

During the Second World War Aberdeen was still a city of workhorses, pulling heavy carts up Market Street towards Union Street, which remains one of the most attractive thoroughfares in Britain.

Country folk would come into town for the Friday cattle market, the wives boarding a tram-car at the Kittybrewster mart and trundling down George Street to alight at the 'Queen' for a day's shopping while their farmer husbands sized up the shape and value of stots and heifers. Women folk would rummage in Raggie Morrison's, the best-known shop in Aberdeen, and treat themselves to a half-crown lunch at Isaac Benzie's, where digestion was ably assisted by the mellow tones of the three-piece orchestra. If there was time, they would take the tram-car back to Kittybrewster (later made famous as the home of Denis Law) to spend a couple of hours in the Astoria Cinema before their menfolks emerged from the Bogie Roll and bonhomie of the cattle ring or the public bar of the Northern Hotel.

As an alternative to the glamour of Hollywood, the ladies might steal away with some secrecy to Whitehouse Street, not far from the Grammar School, where a mysterious gentleman called Jimmy Birnie would read their fortunes and fill their heads with enough dreams of romance to brighten their trauchled lives and send them home to Buchan or Donside or the Garioch on a cushion of air which would sustain them till the next time they came to Aberdeen for the day. Not too many of them would admit to their visits to Jimmy Birnie's little shed in

Whitehouse Street but they went there just the same.

Apart from the conglomeration of cinemas in Aberdeen, mostly owned by the Donald family, there was a most beautiful theatre, His Majesty's, which happily survives to this day, and there we would sample anything from the Shakespearean tones of Donald Wolfit to the rousing tenor of Richard Tauber, whose visit in 1941 still lingers with me as a memorable introduction to the world of theatre. Down at the Tivoli in Guild Street, near the station, the flavour of the old-time music hall was maintained by a motley range of comedians from Glasgow and elsewhere with their supporting casts and an orchestra conducted by Clifford Jordan, who later opened a hotel in Queen's Terrace with his wife Margaret and combined their two names to call it the Marcliffe Hotel.

I remember sitting in the Tivoli Theatre one night during the war, listening to a double act in which the husband, resplendent in bow tie and tails, sang in the most beautiful tenor while his wife accompanied on the piano. They were billed as Ted Andrews and Barbara and a small line beneath their names on the programme read '– and introducing Julie,' their little girl who was yet to become famous as the international musical star of films like *Mary Poppins* and *The Sound of Music*. It all came back to me vividly one evening in November, 1980, as I sat in a bar in Los Angeles, listening to the resident pianist. Suddenly a lady with a familiar face left her drink and crossed to the pianist to ask if she could borrow his piano. As she broke into a magnificent performance of Gershwin music I was in no doubt that this was Barbara Andrews and we ended the evening with a toast to those distant memories of Aberdeen.

Charlie Chaplin had appeared on the stage of the Tivoli in his early days as a comedian and it was one of the special pleasures of my life to take him back in his old age to see the place where he had tried out his baggy pants on an unsuspecting Aberdeen audience at the beginning of the century. But more of that later. So the smell of grease-paint still hung around Guild Street in those days of the forties and fish came strongly from the harbour as open-topped trams went shouding down to the beach from the Castlegate on hot summer days. In streets which fanned out from Castle Street you would find the Aberdeen version of a slum, with the odd drunken woman slavering with a fag at the corner of her mouth and offering herself for a packet of ten Woodbines, which seemed dear at the price. Boys intrigued by the conspiracy of sex would steal off to the New-market and mount the steps to the gallery where a pungent array of stalls included those which sold French Letters, or Frenchies as they were commonly called. If they could not be used for their intended purpose there was always the novel game of filling them up with water to see how much they could hold. I can report from experience that the capacity was absolutely staggering, as proof of a durability which went far beyond the possibility of human performance.

Sometimes there would be a dire event which would send us off with breathless tales on our lips. Such a day began with a grey, damp December morning as the city of Aberdeen lay fast asleep and a piercing shriek rang out over the harbour area to wake folk in nearby Torry. The hour was 2 a.m. But strange noises are not uncommon in the quayside clutter of gangways, sailors, pubs and women of doubtful morals. So those who were disturbed by the shriek turned over in their beds and dozed again till it was time to join the bustle of the fish-houses and the factories. Soon the tram-cars were clanking their way up and down Union Street, past grey granite buildings that stood aloof in the sparkle of first light. Heavy workhorses clopped up Market Street from the harbour to the main thoroughfares. Aberdeen had begun another day. But it was no ordinary day. Shortly after 9 a.m. an elderly man strolling on the foreshore by the mouth of the River Dee was searching for firewood when his eyes set upon an object which sent him gasping to the nearest telephone box to call the police. Later that morning, serious-faced detectives gathered round at police headquarters in Lodge Walk and pondered the mystery of the grisly object. It was a human arm, crudely sawn off, with the fingers arched as if scratching at a killer in self-defence. To this day, more than thirty-five years later, detectives are still asking

the question: Who killed Betty Hadden? To this day I sometimes wonder if I could have helped them.

The year was 1945. The great wartime offensive which had
started with the D-Day landings of 1944 had reached its climax
at Lüneberg Heath in May when Victory in Europe was
declared. By July the inspiration of that victory, Winston
Churchill, had been discarded as Prime Minister even before
the final victory over Japan. It was through that latter part of
the war that I was one of the thirty-six boys at Sillerton House,
where routine was strict.

Morning gong had us out of bed soon after seven o'clock and
breakfast was followed by the mile-or-more walk down Carden
Place, Skene Street and Rosemount Viaduct to school. The
same distance was covered twice at lunchtime and again when
school closed at 4.10 p.m. Tea was followed by 'prep' and by 9
p m. boys of fourteen were heading for bed. Saturday mornings
were for the rugby and soccer pitches and afternoons reserved
for the cinema. After lunch we would line up in the common-
room for the admission money then scamper off down Albyn
Place to a seat in the stalls, to ride away in the excitement of the
Wild West or swoon over Betty Grable or June Allyson. Oc-
casionally the housemaster, George E.C. Barton, would
concede to the attractions of First Division football but, even
when he didn't, his eagle eye was still capable of spotting us on
the terracings of Pittodrie from his own special seat in the
grandstand.

On this particular Saturday afternoon, a cold, late-autumn
day, Aberdeen were playing away from home and the choice of
entertainment was to be the Odeon Cinema in Justice Mill
Lane. Off I set down Albyn Place with two shillings in my
pocket in the company of my friend from Buchan, Alastair
Crombie, whose doctor father had seen me into the world. At
the corner of Holburn Junction we were distracted by a call
from a doorway. It was a sailor asking if we would care to earn a
couple of bob by delivering a message. We would have to take a
letter to a certain house, wait to see if there was a reply and
bring it back to the same place at a given time. Swayed by the

prospect of earning two bob instead of spending it (pocket-money at Sillerton was less than extravagant) we agreed and set out for a district which had a mixed reputation. Down Union Street we went and along George Street, branching into a housing area known as Froghall. It was a slum-clearance district, it seemed, but even then deteriorating into the sort of condition from which the inhabitants had so recently moved. We climbed the communal staircase, gripped by a sleazy excitement in this rather sinister setting so different from our own native corner of the county. Nervously we knocked on the door which was opened by a woman of brittle appearance who took the letter and disappeared inside. From the doorway, a couple of fourteen-year-olds, slightly apprehensive, could see and hear the revelry of a carefree household. The war was over and it was pub-closing time as drunken Servicemen lolled in chairs with women on their knees, exposing legs and thighs and goodness knows what. The woman who took the note returned to say that there would be no reply so we left and hurried back to Holburn Junction for the appointed hour.

The sailor, a smallish, dark, stocky fellow, was already there waiting. We gave him the news and never saw him again. We thought no more of the incident, not even on that December day a few weeks later when I bought an *Evening Express* from Patsy Gallagher's news-stand at the corner of Union Terrace and read about the severed arm. The police were baffled by the discovery. Whose arm was it? Superintendent John Westland, a man of instinct, ordered a check of finger-prints in the police records. It paid off. The prints were those of Betty Hadden, a seventeen-year-old who had once been in some minor trouble. A check at the home of her mother, a certain Kate Hadden whose name was not unknown in Aberdeen, revealed that Betty had in fact been missing from home for several days. But further checks showed that she had been seen at the city's Castlegate on the eve of the grisly find, only a few hours before the piercing noise that rent the northern air. She had been seen with sailors . . .

She had been seen with sailors and she had close friends in

the Froghall district. A youth had been known to carry a message to her, apparently at a dance hall, and the police appealed to the youth to come forward. I knew that I was not that youth, though the description was similar, but from the hazy recollection of the name on the envelope, I had carried a note to someone who could have been Betty Hadden or a friend of hers who had an address in Froghall. The police were anxious to trace sailors and I had a clear picture of the one at Holburn Junction. The case was building up. Alastair and I sat on our secret, nervously protecting ourselves with silence. To admit that the route to the Odeon Cinema that Saturday afternoon had been exchanged for what was possibly an involvement in the prelude to a ghastly murder would have been the likeliest of all short-cuts to expulsion from Sillerton House – and my academic performance was already deteriorating from a starting-point of mediocrity. So the silence was maintained while sailors on boats were followed to the ends of the earth.

No clues were found. The killer of Betty Hadden, it seemed, had done his job quickly, clinically and cleverly. He had probably disposed of the body in a trunk but was unable to tuck in the surplus arm. So he sawed it off and carelessly disposed of it in the river. There were those who believed that the murderer was a local person who knew the lie of the land, a quiet inhabitant of Torry who continued perhaps to live out his life with an air of respectability. The file on Betty Hadden is still there in all its macabre mystery and covered with question marks at Grampian Police headquarters in Queen Street, Aberdeen.

The severed forearm was bottled and labelled for posterity by Professor R.D. Lockhart at the anatomy department of the University of Aberdeen. Several years after his retirement, however, the arm was thrown out in a general disposal of materials at the department, an action which surprised many people, not least Professor Lockhart. It was the last link with the good-time girl with the long, dark hair who will take her very special place in North-East criminal history.

The Press was full of it, of course, and by then I was so intrigued by newspapers that I would stand outside the offices of

The Press and Journal in Broad Street and gaze in wonder that such a plain and shabby building could house the names and traditions of one of the oldest publications in existence. At that time the *Evening Express*, published in the same building, was running one of the most controversial columns of its day, a page of snappy snippets, informative, critical and provocative under the name of Jack Adrian. There were few people in the North-East at that time who did not know of Jack Adrian, whose real identity turned out to be Edward F. Balloch, a Turriff boy who had started his journalistic career with *The Banffshire Journal*, under a noted editor of the day called Dr Barclay, before joining Aberdeen Journals, which was owned by Lord Kemsley. Heading off to London, Eddie Balloch had become the blue-eyed boy of the Kemsley reporting team, covering major events around the world and risking his neck on at least one occasion in order to get his story back to London ahead of his rivals (in those days before television the newspaper 'scoop' mattered a great deal more than it does today). He was following the Duke of Windsor and Mrs Simpson across Europe on one of those interminable train journeys when he tumbled upon a story which had to be despatched at great speed if it was to catch the morning paper. Faced with several hours before the next stop, he jumped from the moving train and ended up with a variety of cuts and bruises – and a proper scoop in the following morning's paper.

In his mid-thirties he was back in his native North-East, apparently being groomed for the top job at Aberdeen Journals, at that time occupied by a wily old bird called William Veitch, who had been a well-known Parliamentary correspondent in his day. In the event, Balloch did not wait for that promotion but all this information was to come my way a few years later when I followed my own determination in defiance of doctors and went in pursuit of my cherished ambition – a job as a journalist.

Chapter Eleven

The Turra Coo

That troublesome heart condition had brought a shaking of heads and second opinions, cardiographs, blood tests and a year of idleness during which I lay helpless in that blistering heat of 1947. The medical message was clearly that, if I were ever to work at all – and that was doubtful – it would have to be in a sedentary position. My own view was simply that, if life was to be as short as all that, I must spend it in the journalism which had been my only choice since childhood.

Glamorous figures like Eddie Balloch had become my heroes but their glossy world of the thirties had been replaced by a post-war austerity in which openings were practically non-existent and firms were struggling to re-employ journalists for whom there was nothing to do because of the newsprint crisis and the consequence of four-page papers. But the *Turriff Advertiser* needed a boy and the persistent pesterings of a loon from Maud, which were already well known to every newspaper in the land, were finally conveyed to the proprietors by John Hardie of *The Press and Journal*.

After months in bed it was a distinct pleasure just to walk again, to breath in the tang of the land and even to raise a protective collar against the Nor'east blast which swept mercilessly over the plains of Buchan and did something to the human character.

The sheer joy of being alive was intensified that March day of 1948 by the prospect of gaining a toe-hold on the profession which had stirred within me dreams of glass palaces. But the Beaverbrooks, Northcliffes and Kemsleys were a distant cry from the joiner's yard which served as the editorial entrance to the *Turriff Advertiser*, through which I passed en route to the most important interview of my life, having travelled the fifteen miles across Buchan by bus. Through the doorway I surveyed an old flat-bed printing machine upon which a chase was being laboriously shuttled back and fore, inking itself on virgin sheets of paper which were in turn whisked into a neat pile by a fly-leaf. There I gazed upon the fundamentals of printing and from there I was directed upstairs via a wooden contraption which opened on to the composing room, where one man sat at the solitary type-setting machine. Two others were picking type from boxes, as we had done as children, and spelling them into words in slotted handgrips. There was an atmosphere of molten lead and slow but certain industry as setting got under way for the weekly issue on Friday. One small corner was partitioned off and marked 'Editor' though I hesitated to enter in case it was merely his W.C. Much as I wanted to meet the gentleman, I preferred to start the interview unflushed! The room was of appropriate size, with one seat and an abundance of paper but it was nevertheless the editor's room, his inner and only sanctum, strewn with papers and proofs, paste and scissors, a cold cup of tea and an ashtray of dottle. From the midst of the clutter there emerged the editor, his eager eyes popping out of thick glasses as he focussed on the intruder who had disturbed his daily doze. He turned out to be an Englishman with a fine moustache, a dainty wife and new-born twins but the power of hire and fire lay with the proprietor, William D. Peters, who strode in with brown hat squarely on his head, pipe just as squarely in his mouth and bree oozing freely from the weeks.

'Ye're wantin' a job?' he confirmed gruffly. 'Can ye dae shorthand?' I had to confess that I couldn't. 'But I'll soon learn', I replied hopefully. A laconic exchange ended in a mixture of pathos and comedy with the old man turning to his son Bob, a delicate man who had crept unnoticed upon the proceedings, and saying: 'Well, what dae ye think?' 'Oh, I suppose he'll dae a' right,' was the opinion which summed me up as a definite risk but one which could, with a little daring, be taken. Persistence pays off in this life so I landed the job and travelled back to Maud, elevated out of my skin to a cloud of joy, which says a lot about my condition considering I was travelling in one of Burnett's old buses. I wouldn't have called the King my cousin. 'Foo muckle are they gyan' tae pey ye?' was my father's first question, having never regarded it as anything but 'a damned tippence-ha'penny bugger o' a job' at the best.

Pay me? Nobody had mentioned paying me anything but what was money anyway? The world was obsessed with it. Well, for a start it was the stuff you paid landladies with and that taught me a fundamental lesson in life – that there is nothing like hard economics for bringing a man to his senses.

That Sunday night I settled in the household of Jim Anderson and his wife Mary at 31 Woodlands Crescent, Turriff, and felt that the world was not such a bad place after all. Mary was a homely woman of ample girth and rosy cheeks from being brought up on the Hill of Tollo, where only the hardy survived. Jim was one of a breed, lean, pale and wiry, a man of considerable knowledge and intelligence who should have been in a job of some responsibility. Instead he was a labourer, sometimes digging roads, sometimes in the harvest field, but ill at ease with his lot and finding some consolation in the *Daily Worker* which he read avidly. He was also a keen betting man, in common with many other people in Turriff, which was surely one of the most gambling-ridden towns in the land at that time. Jim would place a regular and judicious bet and make knowing forecasts that a fourteen-year-old apprentice jockey by the name of Lester Piggott was going to be one of the greatest riders of all time. Whatever one might have said about the *Daily Worker*, there was no denying the skill of its racing tipster. Jim's enthusiasm, however, was no greater than that of his wife who knew a horsey better than most. She depended on more Right Wing sources for her information, thoroughly disapproving of her husband's interest in the 'Worker'.

On my first night, Jim and I settled down at opposite sides of the fireside to take a long, broad look at the world. Real chief-like we were with our grand gestures and sweeping statements and me, at last, a worker with sixteen years of life behind me and therefore equipped with all the answers to life's problems (the doubts come later). We involved everyone from Jesus Christ to Robert Burns in establishing the brotherhood of man, which was coming yet, for a' that and a' that, and it might have seemed only a matter of time before we raised the Red Flag on the Braes of Turra. But the revolution never did materialise and all that happened was that W. D. Peters looked round the door of the editorial doocot and said that he had not mentioned pay but he would wait until the end of the week to decide what I was worth. That attitude, however bluntly put, was wholly in line with my own idealistic view that a man's reward in life should be linked with his value to society. If I were ever tempted to desert a noble opinion it was at the end of that first week when my worth was assessed at thirty shillings, less 1s 11d for National Insurance, which left 28s 1d to pay Mrs. Anderson (35s), bus fares home at the week-end (2s 6d), not to mention pocket money. It took no great feat of accountancy to deduce that I was a pound out of pocket before I started, which could hardly be described as nature's incentive to personal saving. But my father, whose hard head was offset by a generous heart, undertook to make good the deficit and I was soon immersing myself in the life of a country newspaper with the financial problem at least temporarily solved.

Ronald Scott Hutton, the editor, found me a willing worker, running round the town, upstairs and downstairs as often as Willie Winkie, eagerly ferreting out the items which made up the *Turriff Advertiser* every week. If I should be found lacking in a knowledge of death or whist drives (is there a difference?), police courts, Women's Guilds or cattle shows then it was not for the want of experience. On my first week Ronald Scott Hutton sent me to collect some details about an elderly gentleman from Duff Street who had been called to higher service. A kindly lady showed me into the best room in which the dim light from drawn curtains was made even dimmer by the fact that I had just come in from the sunshine. As she went to fetch a closer relative I leaned gently against the sideboard and hastened to readjust my eyes to the light in the room. One by one I picked out the dining table, tea trolley, pictures, sideboard ... SIDEBOARD? I was leaning on it was I not? My sudden swerve of verification was met by the waxen face of a man I had never seen alive but who was finding it not too late for a faintly amused smile at my expense. In the lily-white calm of his coffin he must have seemed just that degree nearer to life than the chattering object which shot out to the lobby to be met by a bewildered relative, who had all the details jotted down on a piece of paper. I left with scarce a word of thanks and returned to our editorial doocot, a trembling slip of a boy, having learned a little sooner than I would have chosen that life on a newspaper is not all gloss and glamour. Hawking the town and countryside for twelve or fourteen hours a day, however, was mainly a joy, even at the subsidised level of thirty bob a week.

Ronald Scott Hutton spent his time in the office, writing feature material but in between times he would break off to relate some of his weird experiences in the East during the war, which was nearly three years past. He would tell of terrible things that happened at the docks when ships came in and there was the tale about the donkey in the Middle East and off I would go on my rounds, bewildered by some of his fantastic stories.

But a most unholy row blew up one Saturday morning between W. D. Peters and Ronald Scott Hutton with the result that the little editor made such a hasty departure that I never did see him again. It took time to dawn on me that following Monday when I turned up for work that I was now, to all intents and purposes, the editor of the *Turriff Advertiser* at the age of sixteen. Among the pleasurable discoveries I had made in my short time at Turriff was that the Balloch family had a financial interest in the paper and that Eddie Balloch's mother, who lived in the town, was proud to open up her scrapbook to show me the evidence of her son's escapades. From the distance of Aberdeen he himself proceeded to bolster my juvenile editorship by supplying some splendid material to help the family out. He sent a provocative series about bygone days in the town, written in longhand, with a note of guidance and encouragement. When the reality of my new-found status finally dawned, I was not averse to stretching back on a chair, putting my feet on the desk and drawing heavily on an imaginary cigar. I would emphasise a point to my sylph-like secretary and summon one of my lackeys from the far end of the room to fly to Foggieloan (all of seven miles away) on a dangerous assignment. It was a creditable performance but the show was soon over when I realised that I had an admiring audience of two office girls at an upstair window across the lane. Reporting duties of the Hutton era were now extended to feature writing and sub-editing. On publication night, which was Thursday, I stayed behind to help fold papers as they were churned from Robbie Cameron's flat-bed machine. When the process ground to a halt in the dead of night and Turriff folk were dreaming about who would win the 2.30 at Newmarket, I tramped round the streets in the cold, dank hours of Friday morning, leaving bundles of 'Advertisers' at shop doors. Then I would head home to Mrs Anderson's in Woodlands Crescent, drop into bed and hardly have time to reflect on this tough but exciting life before drifting into the blissful sleeps of youth.

The big event in the social calendar was the Turriff Show, one of the biggest and best agricultural events in Scotland. It took place, and still does, on the first Tuesday of August when the cream of cattle, horses, sheep and poultry would gather from far and wide to be groomed and pampered, judged and paraded for all of 20,000 people to see. Stock pens were ranged on one side and rows of agricultural machinery on the other and throughout the forenoon the bustle of activity would rise with the morning sun, stockmen in their white coats holding high the aristocratic heads of Aberdeen-Angus bulls which would collect their pedigree prizes, to be proudly displayed alongside other 'firsts' collected at New Deer or Tarland or even the Royal Highland Show, and would surely go on to complete the triumph at Keith on the following Tuesday. By now the town's folk and villagers and others whose knowledge of the finer points of animal progeny was confined to a fillet-steak on a dinner plate came trekking down the brae to the Haughs, which was a splendid natural setting for a public spectacle. They would come in time for the parade of prize-winning stock, great cumbersome beasts swinging their virility from side to side with total lack of modesty or inhibition. Then the sports programme got under way with the travelling circus of heavyweight athletes throwing hammers, putting shots and tossing cabers, decked out in obligatory kilts and semmits and emitting great grunts of effort and satisfaction as their implements took off in various directions. Side by side with brute strength, little madams in kilts and ruffles stepped on to a board supported by lemonade boxes and competed for Highland Dancing medals, all very colourful and coquettish and entertaining if you like that sort of thing but conducted with a deadly seriousness which was almost frightening, especially if you were a judge and fell foul of some of the mothers. They tended to be a toughish breed from down-town Aberdeen who found it hard to accept that their dancing darlings might possibly have been out-done by some other fleet-footed flinger.

Turiff Show, like its neighbouring rival at Keith, was a place for horse-racing, not exactly within the rules of the Jockey Club but fast and exciting nevertheless with fearful rivalries among owners who roared terrifying threats at horses and jockeys as they spun around the limited showring circuit. Then there would be novelty displays by trick cyclists and historical pageants presented on moving lorries by ladies of the Womens' Rural Institute; tug o' war teams arrayed their muscular force at either end of an unsuspecting rope and heaved and lifted to the roars and counter-roars of partisan spectators. So there would be cycle races and slow cycle races and musical chairs for car-drivers, then as the day wore late and folk gathered up their belongings and meandered up through the braes of Turriff the scene was left to the younger fry to fill the large marquee at night. There they would dance till the floor-boards dirled to the beat of a thousand feet and the beer would flow and here and there a fight would break out. But at the end of it all, Nature worked her skeely process of human selection and young folk made the excuse of a warm night to wander off, two by two, along the banks of the Turra Burn to kiss and cuddle and God knows what.

I had been there as a child in the thirties and now I was there as a reporter in the late forties, recording one particular show which was washed out by the most torrential summer rain the North-East had seen this century. Bravely the organisers carried on through a limited programme, led by the stout heart of Niven Paterson, but it was an impossible task. The sheer misery of the day was perhaps best conveyed by my father, who was never short of a descriptive phrase and who recalled of the occasion that 'the watter wis rinnin' oot the erse o' ma breeks'. In those days Turriff still had an abundance of witnesses to the most notorious incident in the whole history of the district, the story of the Turra Coo, which put the name of Turriff in newspaper headlines around the world. I had the good fortune to hear it from Bertie Reid, a local auctioneer who had left school in time to become orra-loon at the farm of Lendrum, helping with the job of looking after the famous cow.

It happened in 1913, after Lloyd George had introduced National Insurance to the British public. Robbie Paterson, the farmer at Lendrum, near Turriff, and a man of some substance, felt that the new insurance should not apply to farm servants and he made his stand by refusing to stamp the card when it was presented by one of his employees. The law stepped in to impound some item which could be sold to raise the money which Robbie should have been paying and they settled on his distinctive white cow. Foolishly, they took it to the town square of Turriff and offered it for public auction, a much-publicised event which drew out large crowds and offered a splendid opportunity for a riot. That opportunity was not ignored and in the ensuring disorder the auctioneer was pelted with a hail of divots and assorted missiles, the police sergeant was struck on the eye with an egg, fireworks were let off and the bewildered cow released to run free.

Finally, it was taken to Aberdeen and sold through the

auction ring but a group of farmers traced the animal and brought it back to the town square of Turriff, where the riot had taken place. Headed by the Turriff Brass Band playing 'Jock o' Hazeldene', the cow was paraded before a crowd of 4,000 people, with anti-Lloyd George slogans on its flanks, and there it was handed over to Robbie Paterson by Archie Campbell of Auchmunziel as a gift of appreciation from his fellow-farmers. The great Scott Skinner wrote a tune called 'The Turra Coo', for that was how it became known, the most famous cow in the world, even if it was not much of a milker, living out its days in peace and distinction till it died in 1919 and was buried at Lendrum where its memorial stands to this day – a memorial not only to a cow but to the North-East farmer who made a notable stand against bureaucracy.

Chapter Twelve

The Rose That Faded

In the still of a summer's day I travelled along the road from Turriff to Fyvie, ten miles away, to interview the head gardener at Fyvie Castle about the abundance of flowers that year. Fyvie Castle was one of the fine baronial halls of Aberdeenshire, the home of Sir Ian Forbes-Leith, a much respected laird and aristocrat. As the gardener conducted me from one profusion to another the conversation strayed to the family and I happened to mention a legend about the Forbes-Leiths which I had heard from older people. The tale was told that a curse had been spoken by a witch-like creature that no direct male heir would succeed to the title. Subsequent history had, alas, borne out the tale. For several generations, succeeding wars had played a part in ensuring that the eldest son had not, in fact, followed his father. But surely, I said in my suspicion of old wives' tales, this was a matter of pure coincidence. Before the gardener had time to air his views, if indeed he intended to do so, we stopped in our tracks as a man in his early twenties came striding down the path towards us, tall, dark and strapping in the Forbes-Leith tradition, as handsome a fellow as you would find.

'Here's young John, the laird's son,' the gardener said hastily.

'The heir?' I queried.

'Aye. The elder of two sons. There are daughters forbye'.

The man around whose head an evil legend hovered was now beside us, with a courteous acknowledgement of the stranger and a warm word of farewell for the gardener. Then he passed on down the garden, followed by the gaze of two silent people. As he disappeared through a gate at the bottom, the gardener was telling me: 'He is with the Guards in Malaya. That was him saying "cheerio" afore he goes back the morn.'

No more was said, and perhaps no more needed to be said, as I hurled back in the bus from Fyvie to Turriff that afternoon. A few weeks later I boarded that bus again, back through the Howe of Auchterless and up the brae to Fyvie Parish Kirk, scarcely heeding the view that spread to the gardens of the castle. For I was back with my Bible to attend the funeral service of John Forbes-Leith of Fyvie. Off he had gone that next day as planned, back to the heat and scent and song of the jungle, to a Malayan land which was deep in the throes of guerrilla warfare. And there, of the bullets and grenades which could have found target on so many thousands of British soldiers, there was one which was labelled for the future laird of Fyvie. From foreign fields they brought him for burial to the land of his fathers, where crofters and labourers joined with the rich and aristocratic to pay their last respects to a fine young man. As the great gathering in the Auld Kirk bowed its head in prayer I raised mine and surveyed the scene. Who would have dreamt of it those few weeks ago? What cloud could possibly dim the sunshine of a perfect summer's day, the joy of a godly garden? I slipped quietly away from the kirk to walk alone to the garden of Fyvie Castle, there to stand on the spot where I had stood before. It was as if time had lost its regularity and I was standing there as though never before, with the earlier visit but an imaginary figment rising now to torment and perplex. There was little knowing and even less understanding of the quirks of fate. But the blooms had faded in that bountiful garden and the wind that blew from a chill airt through the howe came echoing like the eerie call of a witch in the night. At such a time you hardly dare wonder if that evil spirit has had her way once more.

In this day and age when everything is scientifically recorded and computerised it is hard to believe that there were elderly people alive not so long ago who were by no means certain of their precise date of birth. Until the middle of last century they were less particular about birth certificates and the matter was made plain to me when I went to visit Mrs Mary Macdonald at Roseacre Cottage, on the outskirts of Turriff, a splendid old lady who reckoned that she had lived on this earth for a hundred years. Her centenary was naturally a matter of interest to the *Turriff Advertiser*, with telegrams from King George VI and so on, and there she sat with a remarkable clarity of mind recalling details of everyday life in the eighteen-fifties. In a memorable hour of her company I became vividly aware of the day-to-day continuity of time which swept away notions of barriers between the ages and turned all history into a throbbing excitement of the things that happened the day before the day before. . . .

One particular incident of her recollection entranced me more than anything. Mrs Macdonald told me of her grand-uncle, whom she remembered as an old man when she was a schoolgirl. He used to take her on his knee and tell her about his travels which took him to the Battle of Trafalgar in 1805 and there he had actually been present at the death of Nelson. Here was a man who had lived at the same time as Robert Burns, our national Bard, with vivid memories of the seventeen-hundreds, and there was I, talking to someone who had had personal contact with such a man. That simple experience gave me a whole new perspective of time. But the natural instinct of a reporter was not satisfied with the situation of a lady who genuinely did not know her own age so I made some inquiries at the appropriate quarter in Edinburgh to see if there was any trace of her birth being recorded. Indeed there was. Mrs Macdonald had, in fact, passed her hundredth birthday on the previous year and was now into her 102nd year! Taking the precaution of all good journalists, I put a pang of guilt behind me and pre-pared her obituary notice, believing that she would not have many more summers this side of eternity. I tucked it in my wallet in readiness for the day; but I was on holiday in London when I received word of her passing, which could not have been more untimely. I was crossing Westminster Bridge that

afternoon when I paused and extracted the final tribute from
my wallet. On this same spot, I recalled to myself, Wordsworth
raised his head and saw a sight so touching in its majesty. I
lowered mine and dropped the tattered little note over the
parapet, down, down to be carried off by the gilded waters of
the Thames. I permitted myself an ironic smile as it drifted
away, like the lady it described, to the great unknown.

Stories like that of Mrs Macdonald were always good for
regurgitating to the national daily papers where lineage payments could put a fresh complexion on the personal economics.
My connections were with the *Daily Mail* and *Daily Record* but
it was from the *Mail* that I gained a lesson which remains of
paramount importance to every budding reporter: check your
facts. I had not been conscious of any particular lapse when I
received a letter one morning from their head office in Edinburgh which said, in effect: 'When sending us items of local
news please see that they are not copied directly from local
newspapers without checking for accuracy.' I was puzzled.
Why tell me this? There was nothing for it but to ring the
Mail's office in Aberdeen to see if they could throw any light on
the matter. I spoke to Stanley Maxton, a quiet, languid fellow,
shrewd observer and fine writer, who merely chuckled at the
other end of the line as he began to ease my dismay. That same
letter had gone out to all local correspondents and he went on to
tell me the delightful story behind it. Evidently some overzea-
lous fellow, in scanning local weekly papers to find material for
the *Mail*, had tumbled upon a most human and touching story
which was worthy of prominence in any national paper. What a
shame, he thought, that such a gem should be confined to the
columns of a small-town weekly. So he dutifully removed it
from its local setting and re-told it to the *Daily Mail*. It concerned the town bell-ringer who had faithfully rung the bell for
most of his life and had become a well-kent figure to generations. But times were changing and the town had decided that
it could no longer afford his services. With regret it was termin-
ating his appointment. A lifetime of duty and devotion was
coming to an end. However, the old bell-ringer belonged to a

generation which cared less about money than about a job well done and he came forward, cap in hand, and offered to continue ringing the bell just for the love of it. The editor of the *Mail* could hardly believe his luck at landing such a wonderful scoop from under the noses of the *Express* and other popular papers. He was not so charmed with life, however, when he learned the real story. Certainly the old gentleman had done all that was said of him. Certainly there would have been no harm in the enthusiastic reporter taking the story from the local paper. But it would have helped to simplify matters if he had noticed that the column in which this human tear-jerker appeared was headed: ONE HUNDRED YEARS AGO.

Chapter Thirteen

On Top of Her Ladyship

I had now lived through that early post-war period when food was still rationed. Sir Stafford Cripps, a brilliant man in many ways, had become the symbol of miserable austerity in his roll as Chancellor of the Exchequer. Everything was under the strictest control. Motor cars were of the pre-war vintage and I can remember the excitement in the streets of Turriff when someone acquired the first of the new Jowett Javelins. A world which had been hemmed in by the most appalling war in all history and an aftermath of depression was crying out for an escape to freedom. Back in Turriff old Willie Peters had his own minor economic dilemma; by 1950 he was due to pay me the princely sum of £3.00 a week but that was the starting-point for income-tax so he came up with the ingenious solution of paying me just £2.19s. In that way, he said, I would lose nothing and he would save the shilling which would normally have been paid to the Inland Revenue. All was well. But at the age of nineteen and after two-and-a-half years in Turriff I was now ready for the wider world of journalism and that meant turning my eyes once more to the offices of Aberdeen Journals which, despite their dingy appearance, represented the urgency and excitement of the daily paper. There was a fine sense of history about the building which housed *The Press and Journal* and the *Evening Express*, the creaky staircase and the musty smell of the old library and the fact that Robert Burns himself had once visited the place. Side by side with the past came the modern bustle and energy, the daily need to write tonight what would be read in the morning. The corn might still be growing out of my ears but I was filled with a new-found enthusiasm.

The essence of Aberdeen had already been absorbed during my days at Gordon's College – the cold welcome of the granite; the noble sweep of Union Street, its imaginative construction on top of arches putting Aberdeen a century ahead in town planning; the thin voices of the waitresses, the waft of fish from the market and smoke from the Joint Station; the adjacent array in Rosemount Viaduct of the Public Library, the South Church, His Majesty's Theatre and the old Schoolhill Station, more easily remembered as 'education, salvation, damnation and railway station'. Aberdeen was clean and clinical. Its hospitals were set where hospitals ought to be set, in their own grounds and far from the sort of muck and pollution and noise which must have made places like Glasgow Royal Infirmary something of a doctor's dilemma. *The Press and Journal* was set in Broad Street, which happened to be one of the narrowest streets in the city, but even Aberdeen must have its little jokes.

I found myself part of a reporting staff which was a good mixture of experienced older hands like John Dunbar, energetic ones in their twenties, like George Hutcheon, Jimmy Menzies, Jimmy Lees and Ethel Simpson and a few chaps just down from university like Peter Chambers and John Lodge, who was to become a special friend. One fellow asked me where I had come from and when I said Turriff he looked at me as if I might be the Turra Coo itself and said 'Good God, another junior? It's experience they're needing here'. I cleared my throat of a turnip and apologised for the straw in my left lughole. His long scarf, I may say, was dangling invitingly near his thrapple; but mercifully he was an exception.

At *The Press and Journal* and *Evening Express* there was such an array of talented and experienced sub-editors as has ever graced a British newspaper, men of the stature of Sandy Meston, Jimmy Gilchrist and Jimmy Grant, intellectual self-educated giants like George Ritchie and Andrew Ingram, a man with a fine bald dome who had worked in India at the time of Eric Linklater and who taught me once and for all the essential difference between my split infinitives and my dangling participles. They were men who shaped a newspaper with speed and efficiency, gaining the final accolade as Scotsmen extraordinary by working through Hogmanay Night up to the midnight bells, laying down their pencils to rise and shake hands and wish each other 'A Happy New Year' before resuming work on the issue of January 1, which was still a publication day in those earlier times. At quieter moments in the dead of night they would stretch back in their chairs and recall great events and memorable men who put them into words. There were stories of many a notable reporter who would spend his life between the office and pub, including one John Sleigh, who dressed immaculately in black coat, tie and bowler and never failed to add the final glow of perfection from within. No one knew for certain how long John had been in newspapers but his working years had certainly stretched back from the Second World War to the Tay Bridge disaster of 1879 and maybe further. Much whisky and soda had flowed under the bridge since he first put pen to unsteady paper. His timelessness was once reflected by a colleague who wrote a parody of John Sleigh to the tune of 'John Peel'. A typical stanza ended:

And when the Ten Commandments got their first big shak'
  He gave Moses half-a-column in the mornin'

John was tailor-made for society weddings and funerals. On one occasion he was sent to report on the burial of a well-known aristocratic lady from Deeside whose age had long remained a mystery. John was despatched with express instructions to glance at the coffin lid which, in Scotland, had always carried the name and age of the deceased. But John had adjourned to the local hostelry before the interment and was amply lubricated before joining the mourners at the graveside. He was idly listening to the words he had heard so often before, when the finality of 'earth to earth, dust to dust' jogged him into the hazy realisation that he had not looked at the coffin lid. Elbowing his way through the assembled dignitaries, raising his bowler hat in apology, John got down on hands and knees to peer into the grave. It was at that moment of poignancy that John Barleycorn tipped the balance for John Sleigh and sent him toppling headlong on top of her ladyship in her last resting place. The living were appalled and there was, to put it mildly, a sequel back at Broad Street. Canny Deeside folk were thoroughly amused, however, and some winked and said it was the first time her ladyship had ever had a man on top of her; such a pity the opportunity had arrived when she could no longer respond. Older men swore the tale was true and they proceeded to tell another which proved that John Sleigh survived his premature entry to the grave, even if it brought him deep disgrace. Once again John was despatched to Deeside, for a society wedding this time, and not seeking to break the habit of a lifetime he topped up with some human anti-freeze before adjourning to the church. But nature has its necessities and John had to decide which side of the church the bride and her father would traverse when arriving for the ceremony. Having decided, he then chose the opposite side as the venue for his relief. But alas the judgment was at fault. As the bride walked sedately with her father along John's side of the kirk, the inimitable journalist doffed his bowler hat as a mark of respect and an attempt at camouflage and there he stood, eyes fixed ahead, with the dignity of a soldier holding to his post in the face of adversity. Nothing finer had been seen since the Relief of Mafeking.

But the characters of journalism had not all passed away by 1950 (if indeed they have passed away even now) and it was my great fortune to have close encounter with at least one of them. You reached him in a glory-hole into which no light was allowed to penetrate, a dingy, mysterious room piled high with papers and reference books, galley proofs and a general disorder that had the pungent smell of age. There he sat, a fine Dickensian figure, his bulky outline slumped in a chair, long straggly hair sprouting over his ears and disappearing over the collar of an old raincoat which he wore incessantly, or so it seemed. His name was Allan Taylor and it saddens me to think that it will mean little to any but a few. For if Robert Boothby should have been in the thick of world politics, Allan Taylor should have been one of the legendary columnists of Fleet Street or editor of *The Times*. Here was a great conglomeration of humanity built into one man, the shrewdest brain I ever encountered, keen, perceptive, with a mischievous sense of humour, a resounding voice and a large face which the world would have judged as ugly but which was such an adventure of character elements as to make it a study in itself. But it was the wisdom of that head which intrigued me most of all, the brilliant thoughts which leaped out through an eloquent tongue, not only for the benefit of men like Boothby, who valued his opinions more than most, but for young reporters like Jimmy Kinnaird and myself.

If we worshipped at his feet it was because we knew we were unlikely to meet his kind again. A fondness for the bottle had blighted his early career and there he was, not in the higher echelons of Fleet Street but in the comparative obscurity of Peterhead, that wind-blown town on the North-East coast where the choice of Scotland's criminals are sent to cool off for anything up to a lifetime. His job was the editorship of *The Buchan Observer*, a journal he enriched with a standard of writing hardly known to any other local paper in the land. That the powerful prose of such a mind had to share pages with whist drives and fish prices, circulating to a few thousand people in one small corner of Britain was ludicrous. All Britain should have been sharing in his puckish humour, every politician exposed to his analyses and proddings of pomposity. He was as much at home with politics and philosophy as he was with music, art and the dramas of Ibsen but the subject above all which fascinated him as player and writer, as it did Neville Cardus, was cricket. He perceived in the game a whole range of standards and qualities which he could portray as a basis for living. Allan Taylor was the son of plain folk who apprenticed him to a lawyer's office in Aberdeen as the best they could do for a clever boy. In his musty den he would tell me of a peculiarity that dogged his early life. Even great men must have their phobias and his was a totally irrational horror of being 'tagged'. His lawyer bosses thought he could go far in law but he dreaded being known as 'Taylor the lawyer'. He might have chosen any one of many careers but each one carried a tag and that somehow tethered his spirit. Ironically, the label he dreaded most of all was 'journalist' yet that was what he became, working in Laurencekirk before moving to Peterhead in 1926. There, alas, people were more inclined to discuss his alcoholic than his mental capacity though he mastered the former in the twilight of his days.

He was an elderly man before I knew him well enough to impose upon his time but I sought his company unashamedly in the hope that contact with his electricity might conduct even a modicum of his power into my own being. The opportunity to do so came at the age of twenty when William Veitch asked me to take charge of the Buchan district office of Aberdeen Journals at Peterhead. With the help of two other reporters, Andrew C. Buchan and Gordon Argo, I covered the local scene from councils and courts to football and fish prices, working till all hours and sometimes tailing off a long day in the office overlooking the Broadgate, eating a fish supper from Luigi Zanre's and listening to Pete Murray on Radio Luxembourg. As often as not, however, you would find me in the company of Allan Taylor. There were nearly fifty years of difference in our ages but the power of his personality overcame all, the vast geography of his face creasing to reveal a few decaying tusks, his eyes dancing with original mischief. He would tell great tales of local political battles in the twenties and thirties, of the coming of Boothby and the antics of the foxy little Socialist, Max Schultze, a brilliant man of German birth who found himself, invidiously, in the role of Peterhead's Provost in 1939 as we went to war with his native country. (His herring-curing family, disliking Prussian militarism, had moved from the Baltic to live in Peterhead about 1885 and the richness of his culture came partly from his grand-aunt, Malvinia von Meysenbug, the poetess who befriended Richard Wagner and was buried in Rome beside two more of her friends, Shelley and Keats.)

Then Allan Taylor would go farther back to his days at Laurencekirk when he had travelled by train to Stonehaven to attend courts and council meetings, returning in the late afternoon. One aspect of those days stuck firmly in his mind. On the return journey, schoolchildren from Mackie Academy used to join the train and drop off at their various stations. Often they would share his compartment, joking, jostling youngsters always up to their tricks. But in the melee there was one boy who was noticeable as the outling, the quiet one who did not enter into the fun. So he became the butt of many a prank and other boys would hold his head between his knees all the way from Stonehaven to Fordoun. Allan Taylor took special note of the quiet boy who accepted punishment with such good humour, smiling philosophically as if he had some hidden advantage over those bantering youngsters. The lad had big ears and seemed to have them poised for the sounds around him, listening and absorbing. Then a compositor would burst in with an interruption and we changed the subject.

'Why have you never written a book?' I used to challenge him. 'You have so much to offer and your style of writing is so readable.'

'I've tried my hand at plays, three-act ones,' he would say, 'but I can never get past the second act.'

'But the novel,' I said. 'This area is crying out for a book. Why don't you write it?'

He leaned back heavily in his chair and surveyed me as if I had just unveiled one of his secrets.

'I haven't told many people but I did once begin. Yes, I thought I was writing rather a good book about this North-East corner; a novel it was, just the sort of thing you have in mind. That was back in the early thirties, just about the time you were being born, laddie.'

'And what happened to that?'

'Well a peculiar thing happened. I was just about finished when a new book appeared on the market, a novel about the North-East of Scotland. It was called *Sunset Song* and it was written by Lewis Grassic Gibbon. Well man, I read that book and I read it again and I realised that everything I had been trying to say about the North-East had now been said a great deal more eloquently by Grassic Gibbon. So I tore up the manuscript and I've never tried writing another novel.'

I was pondering the misfortune of one brilliant writer having unwittingly thwarted another, when Allan Taylor was speaking again. 'Man, there was just one thing I forgot to tell you. Remember the boy in the train, him that was aye listening and watching? Well I did take the trouble to find out his name. It was James Leslie Mitchell and I need hardly tell you that that turned out to be the real name of Lewis Grassic Gibbon.'

Sunset Song had been followed by *Cloud Howe* in 1933 and *Grey Granite* in 1934 and by the following year, while barely thirty-four, Grassic Gibbon was dead, having failed to rally from a stomach operation. So a great voice of Scotland was silenced for ever, except for an echoing legacy of words and story which the public is only beginning to elevate to its proper place in literature. Allan Taylor's story sharpened my interest in the North-East's greatest writer. Apart from reading his books I came to know his widow, Rebecca, his brother John and several of his friends. Not least, I went on a private pilgrimage to Arbuthnott Kirkyard with his old schoolmaster, Alexander Gray, who, just as my own great-grandfather had fostered the talent of Bertie Forbes, encouraged the young Mitchell when he showed signs of a talent for writing. He was just the boy from the little croft of Bloomfield up the road, come of hard-working country folk who were hewers of wood, drawers of water but seldom readers of books. Old man Mitchell had been scandalised that a son of his should want to write for a living instead of following the tradition of the land and doing something useful. But Alexander Gray took me back to his own house in Stonehaven and turned out a school exercise book which he kept to the day he died and which showed clearly that there were no two careers for James Leslie Mitchell. He was only twelve when he wrote this piece of description in an essay. Little wonder Alexander Gray blinked when he read it: 'What an irresistible feeling of power comes when, on a calm clear night, you gaze up at the millions of glistening worlds and constellations which form the Milky Way. 'Tis then, and then only, that one can realise the full power of the Creator and the truth of the wild dream of the German poet. There is no beginning, yea, even as there is no end.'

The words of an untutored country loon aged twelve! Gray took pride in giving the boy the books which would help develop his talents and took equal pride in telling me about the success of his old pupil. Away he had gone from school to be a reporter in Aberdeen and Glasgow. But his interest in prehistoric times led him into the forces so that he could travel to the Middle East. Years of obscurity at least gave him time to ponder the past and study the relics and finally to turn out a dozen books.

Grassic Gibbon returned to his native North-East and had a reunion with his brother John, a man of no literary leanings at all who chaffed him about his writing and threw out a challenge which can hardly be discounted in any appraisal of Scottish letters. 'With all this damned writing you do, Leslie, why don't you write about your own homeland?'

Leslie just laughed and said aye, maybe it wasn't a bad idea. Whether or not he had it in mind already, he went straight back to his base in Welwyn Garden City and turned out *Sunset Song* in six weeks. It became the first part of the now famous trilogy called *A Scots Quair*. He was already the acquaintance of men like H. G. Wells and by 1934 was making his way as a successful writer. That summer he came north for what was to be his last visit to his native land. By now he had a car and his father's disgust at a son who had chosen a worthless career now turned to sarcasm about 'getting up in the world', with a fine motor car and rising above his old father. There was no pleasing old Mitchell so Leslie spent much of his last visit with Mr and Mrs Gray, who had now moved to Echt, and there in the schoolhouse garden, during that fine clear summer of 1934, he put the finishing touches to *Grey Granite*. Sitting in a deck-chair out on the green he closed his notebook and said, 'Well well, Mrs Gray, that's the end of *Grey Granite* but I dinna expect you'll think as much o't as you did o' the other two.' He drove off back to London with his friend Cuthbert Graham, later to be features editor of *The Press and Journal*, back to his publisher and back to a stomach operation which seemed like a routine matter. Tragically, he did not regain consciousness on the operating table. They brought his ashes back to Arbuthnott Kirkyard, just down the road from the school where he had shown that first glimmer of genius, and there we were, the dominie and I, standing at the headstone and reading the epitaph:

> The kindness of friends
> The warmth of toil
> The peace of rest

words from that closing passage of *Sunset Song* which can move a man to tears. Scottish poetess Helen Cruickshank was there that cold bright burial afternoon in February, 1935, and she described how she looked around at the farming folk who had come from all over the Mearns to see Leslie's ashes interred, wondering whether they would ever understand him as he had understood them. She looked at his father 'with a face like Saint Andrew of Scotland' and his mother with her lined face working nervously, conquering her tears, and she thought of them going home to unyoke the shelt, milk the kye, feed the hens and 'to know the balm that is released from the soil, without knowing that they knew it'.

I am told that old Mitchell realised only when it was too late that he had sired a genius, perhaps Scotland's greatest-ever writer, and he broke his heart as privately as a dour North-East man must, and did not long survive his loon.

From Grassic Gibbon's own place of the sunset Mr Gray turned his gaze across the steaming soil of the Mearns, with its parks and peesies, the folk still working their crofts and the hills beyond. His pupil had given voice to them all. As I followed his gaze across the land so still and enduring I was thinking too of Allan Taylor, himself now gone from a life that had endowed him with gifts but little luck, a life that burned brightly with joy and humour and humanity as a life must if it is to shield itself from hardship. His wife Phyllis was stone-blind but to the end of his day he had cared for her and her house-work with devotion, lightening her days and softening the memory of the brilliant daughter they had bred and reared to academic glory before she wandered one day to a tragic death on the rocky coasts of Buchan. When his blind widow was left alone and helpless she came to live in Maud Hospital, which looked after the aged and chronic sick. I went to visit her regu-larly, feeling that the little attention was at least a token return of the debt which could never be repaid. One day, breaking off from reminiscences of her childhood in Egypt in the eighteen-eighties when her father was helping to build the Suez Canal, she gripped my arm and said she had never visited her husband's grave. On the following Sunday I drove up to the hospital and said we were going to Peterhead. With a firm grip of Allan Taylor's silver-topped walking staff she seated herself in the car and we motored the fourteen-mile journey to the cem-etery. Alas, I was to discover that, among all the headstones and fancily-carved memorials to so many ordinary mortals, there was none to mark the last resting place of Allan R. Taylor. Such is the way of things. But a helpful attendant consulted the record books, led us to the appropriate pathway and then, pacing so many steps forward and so many to the left, said: 'He should be just about here.'

Phyllis Taylor knelt down on the dewy sward and held her own communion with the man who shared those turbulent years. When the two of them had had their say she plucked some greenery from the plot and we formed a posy of flowers and weeds which I had gathered around the cemetery; and there we left Allan Taylor to his anonymity and walked arm in arm, feeling it some consolation perhaps that, in the spreading forest of granite slabs, a great man should be in death as he had been in life – so different from the crowd, so free from that dreaded tag which might have labelled him as lawyer or poli-tician or journalist or even as 'deceased' on a headstone. Such rare human beings do not die while there are those with a moment to remember them.

Chapter Fourteen

Aikey Fair

When the Government engaged Doctor Beeching to apply a surgical knife to the railway lines of this country they went a long way towards cutting the heart out of our village life. For the station was so often the focal point of local activity, the main artery to the outside world. Five trains each way per day brought papers and post, commercial travellers and lowing calves, all in the name of the London and North-Eastern Railway. There was a bustle and excitement at train times for Maud was the junction where the carriages from Aberdeen split into two sections, the one heading for Peterhead and the other for Fraserburgh. Porters would dyst along the platform, calling 'Maud, change for Fraserburgh', and checking carriage doors which were marked 1st and 3rd, for these were deemed to be the classes of rail travel in the days of the steam engine. The fireman sweated black rivulets as he shovelled coal from his tender into the furnace on the footplate to keep the train in steam, while the driver, with an air of adventure about him, leaned nonchalantly with an elbow on his side-vent, winking to folk on the platform and cracking a joke before whistling a blast of steam and pulling his locomotive into a laboured movement which gradually gained momentum till it was scudding round some distant bend, sending back hoots of joy and abandon.

Along those parallel lines, as we have seen, the men went off to war and the wounded came back; children came from Auchnagatt to Maud School and farmers were transported to Friday markets in Aberdeen. Out of it all grew a folklore about the 'Buchan train' which was taken as a synonym for slow and leisurely movement though, heaven knows, in my young day it

112

covered the twenty-eight miles from Maud to Aberdeen in a comfortable fifty minutes, which was fast enough even by much later standards. One of the great characters of the nineteenth century, a man of athletic prowess called Francie Marcus, once challenged the new-fangled contraption to a race and, while he did not exactly win over the full distance, he vowed afterwards that, 'gin I'd gotten her in the Moss o' Byth, I'd hae gi'en the bugger a red face.' (Thereafter Francie devoted his remarkable energies to the fathering of illegitimate children, being called upon by many a farmer with an unmarriageable daughter to sacrifice himself to the duties of human stallion, in the belief that the lassie could only improve the stock with a sire of such admirable physique. Buchan folk, as I have already indicated, are nothing if not practical.)

Of the stories which grew out of the Buchan train, there is one in particular which tells much about the local character. A commercial traveller from England arrived at the Joint Station in Aberdeen one Friday afternoon, en route for Maud. With time to spare, he boarded the Buchan train, found an empty compartment and placed his brief-case and rolled umbrella on a corner seat before withdrawing to the station buffet for a cup of tea. When he finally returned to the train he found to his surprise that it was now jam-packed with brosey farmers on their way home from the Friday mart. Furthermore, his particular compartment was fully occupied with solid men of the soil, his brief-case and umbrella now dismissed to the rack above. Pulling himself up with controlled indignation, but still as polite as the English tend to be, he said, 'Excuse me, gentlemen, when a man puts his brief-case and umbrella on a seat it rather indicates that he has reserved that seat – at least in the part of the world where I come from.' Whereupon the Buchan farmer in the corner, taking his pipe out of his mouth and surveying the Sassenach with measured disdain, replied: 'Ah weel, my mannie, in this pairt o' the world it's erses that coont!'

So the village life revolved around the railway station, with its John Menzies bookstall and refreshment rooms where you could eat or drink amidst the general buzz of activity. The complex of railway lines spread wide into goods sidings, which came into their own on a very special day during the summer holidays every year. That day was Aikey Fair – the first Wednesday after the nineteenth of July – when all roads led to the wooded hillside called Aikey Brae, two miles out of Maud on the way to Peterhead. Aikey Fair was a piece of local history on which I was first instructed by my mother one steaming hot day in 1935 when she took me for a picnic on the embankment overlooking the station. As we tucked into the delicacies of the picnic basket, we watched wave after wave of Clydesdale horses with foals nibbling at their sides as they trekked round the hillside into the village and up the short incline to the station below us. There were scenes of frightening excitement as porter billies, more accustomed to spouting Labour politics than handling animals, struggled with beasts that were sweir to surrender their liberty to the claustrophobic trucks which would take them away to the south. I learned from my mother that they had just been sold at Aikey Fair and I learned, too, the fascinating legend of how it all began.

Somewhere in the mists of history, the story went, a packman was crossing the River Ugie as it flowed from Maud to Old Deer when his foot misjudged a stepping-stone and splash! – he was as far up to his neck as the Ugie will take you. 'A day's business lost,' he cursed as he emerged from the burn like a drookit rat and spread out his wares, as well as his own clothing, to dry. Then country folk came passing along the dusty track nearby on their way to this place or that. When they spotted the packman they stopped for a chat and a view of his colourful wares, for it was not in the nature of those times to pass a man by without at least a greeting, unless he belonged to the horde of beggars who roamed the countryside and terrorised decent folk in those days. Far from being a beggar, he was a genuine trader, perhaps the grand-forefather of the high-powered salesman. As the crowd grew and grew that fateful July day he sensed a most capital opportunity for business. It is said that he sold and sold till, dammit man, he sold his own wheeling drawers before gathering up an empty pack and announcing that he would be back next year, same time, same place. He was as good as his word and, without the preliminary of a dooking, spread out his wares for another day's lucrative business. Word spread from parish to parish in the way of those times and as more people came to buy, more came to sell. It extended up the hillside, known as Aikey Brae (Oakey Brae, the Scots word for 'oak' being 'aik') and soon became an annual fair of increasing importance, the occasion for buying and selling everything from horses to hairpins, settling accounts, taking a hairst fee and clinching them all with a dram. By the middle of last century a short corn in the cap or button-hole had become a sign that a man or woman was out for a fee, with men capable of scything or stackyard work being engaged for the harvest at a substantial £6 to £7, women to gather at £3 to £5 and stout lads to ca' the carts up to £5. Where the crowds would gather you were sure to find the showman so the serious business became levened with all the fun of the fair. Aikey grew to be one of the biggest horse markets in the land, attracting dealers from far and near and there I was, hearing the tale of its beginnings and watching the wise, melancholy creatures being cajoled into their trucks and away to some alien place in the south.

But the story of Aikey Fair does not end there. For many years the show people had arrived on the previous week-end to set up their stalls and amusements in preparation for the Wednesday and, just as those country folk of olden times had gathered to see the packman, so did a later generation roll up to watch the show people at work. Then one Sunday in 1926, an astute showman (perhaps a descendant of the old man?) started up his merry-go-round to test public reaction in an area which had a fair respect for its Sabbath. The crowds stood abashed at first, some edging back lest they be drawn into a desecration of the Lord's Day. But the young, not so conscious of their Maker and itching to have a spin on the roundabout, gave it a second thought and finally threw in their lot with the Devil. Aikey Sunday was born in an instant. It ran side by side with the Wednesday Fair till the workhorse population began to fall away and the emphasis moved more and more to the preceding

Sunday. It became known as Scotland's most notorious continental Sunday, totally out of character with its setting in a land of Sabbath faces and all the more intriguing because of it.

Looking back on those Aikey Sundays before the Second World War, I remember especially 1939 when the speak was of Hitler and the young farm servants thought it would be a braw idea to enlist or join the Territorial Army in preference to taking a hairst fee. Older men just shook their heads and said they remembered overmuch about the last time, the million dead and the terrible sights they saw in France. The sun brought a sinister warmth to Aikey that faraway Sunday as I made my way round the hill with my father and mother. We could hear the noise of the funfair before we left the village and as we reached Aikey Brae there was a hot and feverish excitement that such an appealing decadence could so invade our pastoral peace. There were the merry-go-rounds and the gypsy fortune-tellers, dark, knowing ladies in long ear-rings, holding a key to the mysterious future; there were chair-o'-planes and buskers, music blaring and petrol engines spluttering out fumes that rose with the smell of fish and chips and Broch candy and mingled with the purity of parched grass and the scent of heather on the hill. Over the face of the brae a few tink pipers were swigging at bottles and squeezing the pigskin in weird echoes that rang out across the howe till it near minded you of Auld Nick in the Kirk o' Alloway. Nearby a group of evangelists, complete with tracts and megaphones, were in feverish condemnation of this whole dreadful deed, this vulgar insult to the Lord's Day, till they hardly left the Devil with a leg to stand on, poor man. For sure, they said, we were all on the low road to hell when up piped a dry-humoured farm servant and said 'Weel weel man, we're gettin' a gran' day for't'. I could hardly contain my excitement at the rare sight of it all. Down in the howe the whisperings of the River Ugie were drowned for a day and across on the other side, where the childe St Drostan had come to preach, there lay the Cistercian Abbey of Deer, which had fallen into disrepair before being taken over once more by the Roman Catholic Church in 1930. In the gaunt shell, the derelict walls now kept their secrets like silent nuns, calm in the consuming wonder of time, frowning perhaps at a pagan festival across the burn yet conceding that there was something to be said for a gathering which somehow strengthened that continuing thread of rural life. How fitting that men and women should come again on some appointed day to the place where their forefathers joined in revels before them, to keep tryst with the spirit of the land and the people that were of it.

The emotional effect on the child was strong as the day matured and the great red sun was rolling down on the surrounding woods, trimming the firs before drowning in the horizon beyond. It was time to forsake the hillside for another year and make for home, so we gathered our stuff and joined in the general exodus and, as a last glimpse of Aikey, we stopped to catch sight of a young man whose name had a ring of magic, Benny Lynch. All Scotland loved little Benny, the boy from Glasgow Gorbals who had so recently been flyweight boxing champion of the world before losing his title through overweight. Benny had started as a slogger at fairgrounds and on the way to the top had gathered too many hangers-on who quickly landed him back where he began. But Benny had spirit. That sunny day at Aikey Fair he sparred forty-eight rounds with Freddy Tennant and at the end of the day, as we started for home, he was calling defiantly to all who would pause and listen: 'I'll be back – and if I get to the top I'll stay there'. But Benny returned to his back-street slums and chums, never to see the top again and to die a few years later, down-and-out and penniless. So the crowds went home that night, fine and red and sonsy and contented, home to milk the kye and bed down for an early start to the moss, there to cut and set the peats for winter's fuel. It was part of a familiar pattern that had known little change for generations.

But Aikey Fair was only weeks past when Hitler's hell broke loose and the crowds did not gather on the hillside again until 1946 when, despite the great rift in tradition and the gloom of austerity, the farmers still came cheerfully with their horses on the appointed day. But the tractor was now dehumanising the farmstead, ousting the Clydesdale from its place of dignity, and the end of Aikey Wednesday was surely in sight. In 1950 I was there as a young reporter to find that the gathering of horses was down to a mere hundred. The following year it had dropped to sixty. I should have been better prepared in 1952, for the end came more suddenly than anyone expected. Back I went with my notebook and pencil to find that no-one had yet arrived except Peter Grant, the hotelkeeper from Old Deer who was also the feuar of the Aikey land. His refreshment tent was already in position, stocked for a moderate day's business. A few buyers arrived from the south on the forenoon train to Maud and came on by hired car to Aikey Brae. Policemen turned up to regulate the traffic, as had always been the custom. Ten o'clock became eleven o'clock and by noon only one piebald pony had been presented for sale. It came from Willie Barber of Aberdeen and it was sold to another well-known horsey man from Aberdeen, George Ross, for £21.10s. In such ludicrous circumstances and after centuries of high spectacle the great Aikey Fair came abruptly to an end.

But it was a warm day and a man's mouth was for more than speaking with so the small gathering repaired to Peter Grant's tent. Big Sandy Wilson from Strichen was there and that was a joy in itself for Sandy was another of the notable characters produced by the Buchan district. In his varied interests and activities, he had been mainly a horse dealer, on such a scale that he once paraded a hundred horses at Aikey.

'What are ye for?' I asked Sandy as we gathered at the bar counter.

'Man, I'm nae in a drinkin' humour – I'll just hae a rum,' he said.

'Rum for Sandy,' I ordered, reaching for the ginger bottle. 'D'ye want something in it?'

'Aye,' said Sandy. 'Mair rum.'

So a large rum it was and he opened his mouth and filtered it straight down his thrapple before I had time to feel grateful that this wasn't one of his drinking days.

Sandy went to Canada on one occasion to visit relatives and regarded the event as no valid reason for depriving the inner man of his liquid comfort. In a state of advanced inebriation he looked up at the moon one night and convulsed his Canadian hosts by declaring 'Man, that's helluva like the Moon we hae in Buchan.' Then back to his beloved Buchan and down in the fishing town of Fraserburgh one Saturday night, he joined the throng in the Broadgate as the pubs were closing. Like many communities that live by the sea, Fraserburgh was given to periodic outbursts of evangelism and there on the plainstones a Salvation Army girl was fair giving Auld Nick a bad name. She testified to her own wickedness before that wondrous moment when she saw the light and some farm servants, down for their Saturday night out, nudged each other and said dammit man, they would rather have known her before the light appeared. If she was half as fervent in the dark she would still have been a fire risk to the haystacks! Her blousy bust gave rhythmic counterpoint to her rantings as she reached a fine and holy climax with the ambiguous declaration 'Tonight, my friends, I am in the arms of life; tomorrow I may be in the arms of Jesus . . .' when up piped Sandy Wilson with fruity voice and rekindled spirit of youth to inquire: 'And what might you be doin' on Monday nicht, lassie?'

But here we were in the dying minutes of Aikey Fair. One piebald pony. The old fair that had started with a footless packman had taken centuries to turn full tilt but now it had served its purpose and was passing just as swiftly as it had come. Those of us present tidied up the loose ends of history and drank a final toast. The Sunday fair still survives and draws upwards of 10,000 people on that Sunday in July but as I walked away from Aikey that Wednesday in 1952 I felt that I had left something of myself on the bareness of a Buchan brae, the part that belonged to older times. As I turned back to gaze on the desolate scene I knew that I was witnessing a poignant moment in local history, for we would never see its like again. Such a moment is hard to crystallise in the hour of its happening. Time alone can give it perspective.

119

Chapter Fifteen

The Lifeboat's Over!

You are not long in the company of an Englishman before you know his whole story, unabridged, unexpurgated. Not so the Scot, least of all the rural Scot and if there is anything less than least it will be the hardy chaps of the North-East. In their granite towers of dumb caution they are dourly suspicious of gab in all its forms. There is the story of the bowler-hatted commercial traveller who boarded the train at Maud and entered a compartment already occupied by two Buchan farmers. In the breezy manner of the highway, the man raised his bowler and said 'Good morning, gentlemen.' The two worthies exchanged looks of contained amusement and merely took another puff at their pungent Steenhives. The commercial did not intrude on their silence for the rest of the journey and settled diligently to his *Scotsman* crossword. When he came to his destination at Ellon, he gathered his brief-case, opened the compartment door and, with normal courtesy, raised his hat again and said: 'Well, . . . good morning, gentlemen.' Still there was no acknowledgement and when the man had finally departed, one farmer turned to the other and summed up the creature with unmistakable disgust: 'A gabbin' vratch!'

Economy in words, economy in most aspects of life, thus the reputation for thrift and the legion of international stories about the mean Aberdonian, most of which originated in Aberdeen itself or twal' mile roun'. But it was based on thrift, not greed, a conviction that a man must make the best of what he had, springing no doubt from the earlier life on a grudging land that had to be farmed with good care and good sense,

120

leaving no room for waste. The whole conditioning of the species made for a certain dourness but it found its own natural outlet in hard work and dry humour and did not swell into a social problem on a psychiatrist's couch. However, for those who might be intent upon probing the inner thoughts and feelings, even for those like myself who grew up with it, there were daunting problems.

Take the religious and political standpoint, for example, and you would soon find out what I mean. On paper the religious position seemed plain enough. The people were mostly on the roll of the Church of Scotland, the doughty Aul' Kirk which stood bare and forbidding on every parish heath. Their visitations upon the building might be twice a year, at the May and November communions, or if they wished to minimise the shock effect of their rare appearances on the poor brute of a minister they might well attend on the preceding Sunday as well. They would tell you they learned the Catechism at school, though they were damned if they could recite it now, and the man body would stump into the kirk like a tethered tup, solemn-faced and slow with the ill-gait of a man entering a place of infamy where he would rather not be seen. His red-faced wife, tight-lipped and douce, would be left to bring up the rear, which might amount to half-a-dozen bairns, to raise her tones at hymn time, bow her head at prayer time and maybe open her purse at collection time. And when it was all over Jeems would dyst his way to the door muttering that it would have been a grand day for riddling tatties. If it had been communion and the wine was served in the microscopic glasses which became the fashion, he might nudge a neighbouring farmer and crack: 'We could hae been daein' wi' something stronger on a caul' day like this.' Then he went home to his chappit tatties and thought little about God or religion till the next communion or the one after that if he was not burdened with one of those unreasonable ministers who threatened to cross him off the list. Of course he would give Jesus Christ innumerable mentions in the interval but seldom in the Biblical context. The trouble with Jeems and Dod was that they distrusted holiness as much as they distrusted gab. They saw it as a doubtful element and would judge harshly any neighbour who dared to profess openly his belief in God. Such a soul was suspected of brain impairment and promptly dismissed as having 'gone all to hell with religion'. Those brave men who took to the ministry in places like Buchan deserved either danger money in this life or a special corner of Heaven thereafter, or both. From the start they were social outcasts, unworldly creatures who would not be much good at pulling neeps, figures of good-natured ribaldry who were the better accepted if they took a dram, in which case they were likely to be voted most capital chaps, 'just nae like a minister ava'', which was taken to be a recommendation.

Perhaps it was the bi-annual tirades about non-attendance which drove people away from the Church of Scotland, for the Scot does not care to be too forcibly reminded of his misdemeanours. But who could blame a minister who preached for fifty weeks in the year to a handful of converted pandrop-suckers if he grasped at the chance of a little straight talking when suddenly confronted by a houseful of half-kent faces? Then again it may have been the severity of the Aul' Kirk service that set the Buchan folk back on their heels – the plain, unpadded pews that would give a man corns where corns were never meant to be, the stark walls and windows and the long theological sermons that too often meant little to hard-headed folk. I can think of Kirsty leaving the kirk one dry summer Sunday when Dr M. Welsh Neilson, the minister, had preached a wise and well-considered sermon on the theme of 'Always keep a well in your own backyard'. He related it to the current drought as a worldly illustration of his real message, which was about the wisdom of keeping within one's self a spiritual well from which to draw strength in times of need. When Granny Barron commended the sermon to Kirsty she responded enthusiastically with the comment 'Aye, Mrs Barron, it is richt handy when ye've a drappie water aboot the back door.' Alas, the spiritual analogy had evaporated in the reigning pre-occupation with a shortage of water.

THE LIFEBOAT'S OVER!

Yet the severity of the service was in keeping with the character of the area and its people and perhaps there was something to be said for the Aul' Kirk form of worship. It may have been stark but wasn't there something wholesome and roundly satisfying about a minister who mounted the pulpit steps and without palaver summoned his flock with 'let us worship God'. That was basic.

Sundays in the thirties were usually spent at your grandparents, in my case at Mains of Whitehill, four miles up the road from Maud. At the foot of the farm road stood the old Kirk of Whitehill, which had been an important place of worship before the motor car took people to village kirks nearby. But it was still in use on one Sunday of each month when neighbouring ministers took the chance of addressing an old sermon to new ears. On the preceding week my grandfather, Arthur Barron, who was in such close harmony with his land, took a pride in seeing that the place was cleaned and made decent for the service, as if seeking to repay his Maker for the many debts of life. Sometimes I was sent along to lend a hand and on those occasions I grasped at the chance of exploring the in-timmers of a kirk when the minister was not there. It was something I had always wanted to do, just as I liked to sneak into my father's rostrum at the mart and pretend that I was selling cattle. When I tired of scrubbing and polishing I would steal away to the pulpit, mount the steps with due pomp and, having set my Bibles round their various positions, proceed to deliver an imaginary sermon to an imaginary congregation before being hounded by a most unimaginary command to come out of there at once and not make such a din in the Lord's house.

It was in the Kirk of Whitehill that I gathered my first memories of preachers. One in particular I recall for he fair could make the rafters dirl as he laid forth about Moses and Abraham and lots of folk I had never heard of. By the sound of them I had no real wish to further the acquaintance either. Yet, looking back, there was a good deal to be said for those spiritual scrubbings. He spoke of hell with absolute authority; indeed, had it not been so far away, I should near have sworn that the man had been there, so clear was his account of fire and furnace. At times its warmth may have caused envy in the cold air of the kirk; but without doubt it had a sobering effect on the potential sinner. It was a brave heart that would have considered anything but the straight-and-narrow in the face of such fiery threats, such technicolour, wide-screen projection of Auld Nick's Palace of Purgatory. Psychologically, the message would not have been uplifting to any but hardy North-East folk, for it labelled them with sins they did not know they possessed and held out a pretty slender hope for improvement. But his congregation was made of steely stuff and he knew that they would not readily give up the ghost, particularly the Holy One, and that they would strive to live, if nowhere else, at least on the lesser slopes of sinfulness. Today the Kirk of Whitehill is no longer a kirk. It became, as I recall it, an enormous henhouse with tier upon tier of clucking, laying hens. In an atmosphere so charged with the power of hell's generators, I am willing to bet there were no more righteous hens in Christendom, laying eggs of golden purity and ne'er coveting a neighbour's nest, nay, nor casting a lustful eye upon a neighbour's cockerel.

But if the rural folk of the North-East had an apparent indifference to religious matters it may simply have been that they felt little need to show it, having been fired by the essence of Christianity for longer than anyone knows. Their code of honest, decent living may well have stretched from prehistoric times when a great Maglemosian horde is believed to have come from southern Europe to settle in the land we now know as Scotland. They were a peace-loving people, we are told, with the basic ingredients of true civilisation, men with a lesson in living which became lost in the developing process of land division. That was before the age of the Savage but, alas, the lesson has yet to be re-discovered. We pride ourselves in our progress as human beings but have we really come so very far from the ways of the jungle? In a few odd corners of the world you can still find remnants of the old civilisations and the

North-East of Scotland could well be one of them. It is just a thought.

How strange that the fisher folk in places like the North-East could march side by side with their rural kinsmen and yet remain a race apart in so many ways. In places like Fraserburgh, Peterhead and St Combs they spoke a language which was scarcely intelligible to farming people just a few miles inland. Their religion was a more complex matter than that of their farming neighbours but much less of an inhibition too. Living by the sea with its attendant dangers had made them more aware of their Maker and the possibility of meeting Him a little sooner than the dysting ploughmen who turned over the fresh soil of inland parks. So the men who sailed away in their fishing boats to reap the harvest of the sea came home on a floodtide of evangelism which found expression in a baffling diversity of religions. In towns like Peterhead and Fraserburgh, with populations around the 12,000 mark, you would find not only four or five Church of Scotland buildings and Roman Catholic and Episcopal ones as well but a whole choice of Baptist, Methodist, Pentecostal, Christadelphian and Salvation Army persuasions, not to mention the Brethren, which divided itself into separate shades of Open and Close and what more I cannot tell. I have sat in some of those places and listened to fishermen and their families give testimony to the day they saw the light and there was no doubting their sincerity. I merely marvelled that people from my own North-East corner, so near to the reticent folk of the land, could speak so unashamedly about their God. Religion was a more conscious matter in the fishing towns and villages where their gable-ends faced out to the mysteries of time and tide, and the tang of the ocean could lure them in search of a lucrative living or just as swiftly despatch them to a watery grave.

I had some first-hand experience of their homes and their hearts one February day in 1953, a few months after I had been asked by William Veitch to move the Buchan office of Aberdeen Journals from Peterhead to Fraserburgh, a town which was then outstripping its local rival in prosperity.

The great January gale of that year had blown itself out just nine days earlier, leaving wreckage everywhere, and the skies had opened to the sparkling clarity of a premature Spring. Overhead a few white wisps of cloud were drifting to nowhere in particular and Fraserburgh was having its after-lunch nap. But far away in the North Sea the storm was still churning up the waters and rippling its effect across a hundred miles. Yawls had sailed out that morning to bring in fresh catches of white fish when suddenly they were caught up in a dangerous swell by the inshore regions. Fraserburgh lifeboat went out to shepherd them home and, with the last one over the harbour bar, coxswain Andrew Ritchie turned his lifeboat back towards port. Skippers know how to ride those rough seas but the great swell which echoed that distant storm was suddenly to throw up a freak sequence of wave movement which could not have been anticipated. Up came a lump of water and tossed the Fraserburgh lifeboat over on her face, trapping the seven crew members inside.

Within minutes the cry had spread through the town: 'The lifeboat's over!' And instinctively a whole population seemed to be running for the shore. Fraserburgh had lost a lifeboat before (and was to do so again) and year by year those people knew the agony of giving up a few of their fishermen to the mysteries of the deep. I am sometimes even today haunted by the plight of those townsfolk as they reached the shore to witness one of the most ironic dramas ever enacted. There I stood among them, the local reporter and one of the first to see crew members fighting for their lives within a few hundred yards of their own firesides. Frantic sons and brothers and fathers had to be restrained from jumping into the boiling surf to reach out a helping hand. The sea was in command that day and would take any other victims who cared to come. In the gurgle of their upturned boat the men tried to swim down and out beneath but their lungs choked up with the water, their bodies were battered in the rage and now those of us who were so near and yet so far could only stand and shout our encourage-

ment. 'Come on, Andrew, stick it, man, stick it!' Andrew
Ritchie, coxswain and powerful swimmer, reached out with his
great arms and thrashed his way towards his wife and young
family, driven to the limits of his remaining stamina. The
cheering rose to crescendo as if for a sporting achievement,
with victory now seemingly in his grasp. Then up bobbed a
piece of flotsam, knocking the very last ounce of strength from
his body – and we watched, helpless, as a brave man went
under for the last time. Five others went the same way and only
young Charles Tait survived. Folk ran this way and that in the
general upheaval, relatives pumping dear ones in the faint hope
of life's glimmer. But the cruel sea had struck again.

That evening I had the melancholy task of visiting the homes
of the dead to collect photographs and biographical details for
the next day's *Press and Journal* and there I was introduced to
the philosophy and steadfastness of the fisher folk's religion if I
did not know it before. Though young Charles Tait survived,
his father was drowned and it was to old Mrs Tait that I made
my first call. There she sat by the side of the coal fire, gazing
into the flames that danced their evil round the room. With a
heavy heart and eyes fixed on the fire, she spoke quietly and
sensibly about the whole disaster. In the sorrow of losing her
life's partner she was able to point out the blessing that it was
the father and not the son that had been taken. She was an aging
woman whose burden might be burden enough but how much
worse it would have been for the young Mrs Tait with her children to bring up. We had to count our blessings, hadn't we? A
week later they called a meeting to enrol replacements in the
lifeboat crew, for a town could not afford to be without its
mercy ship when the livelihood depended on the sea. There
was no scarcity of volunteers. Leading the queue was Skipper
Joe Ritchie, offering to take the place of his brother Andrew.
The survivor, Charles Tait, had brought along his younger
brother who wanted to take the place of their father. It is the
way of things when the sea runs wild in your veins and there is a
job to be done, a tradition to follow. What can you say of such
people?

We packed the Old Parish Church for the funeral service and suddenly the great variance of religious interests channelled themselves into one remembrance, thanking God for the courage and resilience that sent men down to the sea in little ships; giving thanks too for the wives and families who waited and worried, knowing that the friendly waters which lapped their doorstep at the sunset glow of a still evening could just as quickly whip up a furious floodtide of sorrow. Country folk came in from their farms and villages, glad to pay tribute to the neighbours they knew so little but respected so much. I like to think of them together, these two factions of the North-East scene – the pride of the sea, the salt of the earth.

Chapter Sixteen

Lord Jesus to Lord Boothby

If it was hard to plumb the spiritual depths of the North-East,
the task did not become easier when you tried to gauge the political temperature. By tradition, I suppose my ancestors and
most of their neighbours were Liberals, sending to Westminster such distinguished men as Fred Martin, the blind M.P.
from Mintlaw. But when the party lost its fire, they could find
no clear affinity with either the class-consciousness of the up-
and-coming Labour Party or the upper-crust image of the
Tories. Instead they settled for a new phenomenon called
Boothbyism. In their moment of need along had come a handsome young man with an Oxford degree, a good Scottish background, a golden voice and a personality which disarmed the
men and captivated the women. At twenty-four, Robert John
Graham Boothby, only son of a comfortable Edinburgh family,
was heading for Westminster, the brightest prospect on the
political scene, soon to become Parliamentary Private Secretary to Winston Churchill, set fair for unlimited possibilities.
A few Aberdeenshire farmers, headed by Baillie Booth from
Peterhead, had gone to Orkney to buy some bullocks – and
brought back Robert Boothby as an unexpected piece of live-
stock. They had gone along one evening to listen to the young
man as he fought an unsuccessful campaign with the Liberal.
The men of East Aberdeenshire liked what they heard and
judged rightly that he was a man of such independent thought
and action that he would represent them with good sense and
conviction, even if it ran against the grain of his party, which
happened to be the Conservative Party. In other words, he

would reflect their own distinctive character.

Some of my earliest memories concerned the name of Boothby, pronounced with a great many more o's than it was spelled and spoken with a reverence by his local adviser, the late hammer-throwing champion Archie Campbell, who was sometimes in the company of my grandfather and who wrote popularly under the name of 'The Buchan Farmer'. About the time I first remember him, Mr Boothby was wedding himself to Lady Diana Cavendish, from the well-known Devonshire family. A few years later that marriage was dissolved and the folk of East Aberdeenshire winced but granted that his private life was his own, even if divorce was hardly known among the farming fraternity of Buchan at that time. Irreconcilable couples tended to thole each other, no matter how deep and interminable the misery, rather than be dragged into the shame and prominence of the Court of Session. About the same time, when war was breaking over Europe, the so-called scandal of Boothby's connection with Czechoslovakian assets in this country exploded as a storm of international proportions and there, prematurely and tragically, a career at the top end of politics where he most properly belonged was no longer a prospect. In backing a move for Czech assets in this country to be frozen and paid to those exiles whose assets had been confiscated by Hitler, he failed to declare a personal interest in the matter. (It was later discovered that he was not obliged to.) Political opponents did not pass up their opportunity and Parliament ruled that he had brought the House into disrepute. Boothby protested his innocence of any shady work and convinced many people in high places as well as his constituency party, who met him at the height of his crisis with the full expectation of parting company. But the doubt was cast and Churchill, who had seen such great things ahead for the young Boothby, cut him adrift and gave him no further support for the rest of his political life.

It was a sad and saddening experience and left Boothby, whose good nature held little room for bitterness, with some harsh things to say about his old master. If ever a man was destined for Number 10 Downing Street it was surely Robert Boothby. He had many of Churchill's qualities – mental and physical capacity, vision, courage, the power of language; he had perhaps an even more engaging personality than Churchill and was one of those rare beings whose very presence would charge the air with an electricity. Great men can sometimes be a disappointment in the flesh. I remember once losing my way in the House of Commons, finding myself alone in a remote corridor and suddenly coming face to face with the aging Winston Churchill. The whole of his legendary life came flooding in, from the Boer War and the Siege of Sidney Street to his immortal years of the Second World War, his sayings and doings. I was seeing it all in the history books, being read a hundred years ahead by people who would speak of Churchill in the same breath as Cromwell and Pitt and Gladstone. Yet there, in a lonely corridor, it was hard to condense that legend to a size which would fit inside the mortal frame which approached me now. Boothby was a more flamboyant personality than this. Perhaps he lacked stability.

So the forces of history worked against Robert Boothby and the nation's loss became East Aberdeenshire's gain. He spent his days fighting for the fishermen of Peterhead and Fraserburgh, their minimum prices, their grants and loans, and fighting just as hard for the Buchan farmers, their oats and beef cattle, their subsidies and deficiency payments. He made his mark at the Council of Europe but eventually accepted a knighthood and later a baronetcy, which made him Baron Boothby of Buchan and Rattray Head (the land and the sea), still a powerful voice but confined to a roll in public life far short of what it should have been.

As a journalist, I attended the dinner held in Aberdeen to celebrate his knighthood. His old friend Compton Mackenzie was the main speaker, who kept the company in stitches for half-an-hour with a speech that might have been matched only by Boothby himself. Then, his audience soft with laughter, he drove home a telling jab at the 'farce' of the Czech affair. The man who should have been at that moment Prime Minister of

Great Britain had become a public entertainer, empanelled on the cheapness of television games. On that night in Aberdeen and on subsequent occasions when I have sat with him at his home in London's Eaton Square, I could not but reflect on the cruelty of fate. The man himself would take it all philosophically.

When the baronetcy winged him off to the Lords, he left a vacuum which was to become a whirlpool of political trouble in East Aberdeenshire. At first, the constituency, so long accustomed to the uniqueness of a Boothby cult, had to refresh its memory on the party to which he himself belonged. That they would, in tribute, elect a candidate of the same party went without saying. But in the late fifties there were no Boothbys on the political horizon. If they had not already thrown away the mould then men of that rugged ebullience were finding their niche in life outwith the spectrum of politics. East Aberdeenshire settled for an upright young man from one of the aristocratic homes of the district, Patrick Wolrige-Gordon, whose mother was a daughter of the colourful Dame Flora MacLeod of MacLeod, Clan Chief and hostess to her worldwide flock at Dunvegan Castle in Skye. Young Patrick was virtually unknown on his own native heath, having been educated, like most of his aristocratic cousins, in England, treading the familiar path from Eton to Oxford. When the time came, he left a degree unfinished to come back to the land of his birth as Conservative candidate. Out of the speculation as to who would be chosen came this political sapling, introduced to the people by one of his neighbouring aristocrats, Major David Gordon of Haddo, who was later to become Lord Aberdeen. Everything smelled of roses, or so it seemed. Patrick Wolrige-Gordon won the by-election caused by the departure of Boothby and consolidated his position at the General Election of 1959, which followed soon afterwards; then his troubles began to brew, not because the fishermen thought he was not fighting their cause, not because the farmers were dissatisfied or the general mood was turning against him. Trouble was coming from the source which had introduced him, from the upper crust of his com-

LORD JESUS TO LORD BOOTHBY

mittee, from Major Gordon of Haddo and even from his own
brother who was now laird of the family home at Esslemont,
near Ellon. The folk who had worked to bring him in were now
working just as hard to get him out.

The Tories had run into a wave of national unpopularity, by-
elections were bringing disastrous results and the call had gone
out from London to the constituency chairmen to make sure
that their houses were in order. There was a general casting of
opinions, followed by rumours of hush-hush dinner parties for
the hierarchy of the East Aberdeenshire Tories. The outcome,
as later revealed: Patrick Wolrige-Gordon, recently elected
M.P. for East Aberdeenshire, no longer held the confidence of
some of his constituency bosses as the man to retain the seat at
the next election. Executive meetings were organised to bring
about his rejection as candidate and, on the surface at least, it
seemed just as simple as that. But as the whole fester began to
erupt it became clear that another issue was involved, though
no-one was keen to admit it. Young Patrick was now courting
Anne, the beautiful daughter of Peter Howard, author, playwright and leader in Britain of the growing Moral Rearmament
movement. In higher circles there were people who still
thought of M.R.A. in terms of Fascism through the founder,
Frank Buchman. Patrick was said to be spending too much
time on Moral Rearmament and not enough on his constituency though he had previously met his executive and thrashed
out that matter. Was there, then, a rooted objection to the fact
that he was connected with M.R.A. at all? That was what no-
one would admit.

The ordinary folk of East Aberdeenshire were not much concerned about Moral Rearmament, accepting Wolrige-Gordon
for what he was – a decent young fellow who was doing his best
to learn about the problems of the constituency and was prepared to work hard for his people. The plain fact was that very
few Buchan folk had any notion of what the initials M.R.A.
stood for and when they discovered, they were more than
outraged that a young man should be persecuted for what they
were convinced were his high moral aspirations, especially at a

133

time when the Government he served was on the verge of acute embarrassment at the hands of the whores and pimps of the Profumo Affair. There were rowdy meetings and much writhing and wrangling but the outcome of a neck-or-nothing showdown was that Patrick Wolrige-Gordon carried the people with him. It was a hazardous business for a sensitive man still in his mid-twenties, enough to shatter his confidence for years to come. Perhaps it could be said that he had enough moral armament to see him through – though goodness knows what part the ordeal eventually played in his political destiny. The rumpus coincided with his wedding which was attended by a trainload of well-wishers from Buchan, who travelled to Anne Howard's parish in the south of England and joined with people from many walks of life. Patrick and Anne were to find that the loyalty and sense of justice which are built into the Buchan folk would sustain them in their plight. Without the personal support of plain country bodies they could not have survived. Politically, Patrick Wolrige-Gordon continued as an industrious Member of Parliament throughout the sixties but he perished in the spread of Scottish Nationalism which ran down from Moray and Nairn through Banffshire and into Aberdeenshire in the early seventies. I shall leave the political pundits to analyse the root-cause of that particular phenomenon.

Among the Buchan folk I was never aware of any deep allegiance to one political party, except the Liberals in earlier times. Boothbyism had taken care of itself; Socialism was regarded as fine for railway porters and Fraserburgh toolworkers but seemed to suffer from a suspected affiliation with the Devil; and in the general search for an alternative I suppose Nationalism looked as safe a compromise as any. It gave expression to that minority of Scots who held genuine aspirations for self-government and enabled bankers and schoolteachers and people like that, for whom political posturing was a risky business, to take up a stance of some sort. But I doubt if there is a party which can face a General Election in Buchan with feelings of utter safety. Dogmatic doctrine does not exactly clink with the native character.

Chapter Seventeen

From Maud to Moscow

By the time of the Wolrige–Gordon rumpus I had not only moved back from Buchan to the Broad Street headquarters of Aberdeen Journals, having enjoyed the three years in my native corner, but had also moved south to explore the deeper jungles of journalism. I have long wondered what takes us from one place to another in this life. Is it a restless pursuit of money, position, adventure? Are we guided by instinct along the road of a pre-destined fate? Or are we simply the aimless creatures of circumstance? Few of us have more than a hazy notion but for my part I became aware that the time had come to move from Aberdeen if I ever intended to sample the working world beyond.

I had spent the latter part of the fifties as a sub-editor on the *Evening Express*, laying out pages, writing headlines and generally trimming other people's writing to fit the spaces. Broad Street was a busy, exciting place, part of the massive empire of Lord Kemsley (his daughter married the Marquis of Huntly) but soon to pass into the hands of Roy Thomson, an unknown name from Canada who suddenly appeared on the British scene, bought up *The Scotsman*, set his sights on Kemsley's network of regional newspapers and gained the franchise for Scottish Television, drawing upon his experience of television in Canada to declare that he had just been given a licence to print money. How right he was.

Most of my colleagues of the early fifties were still there, some of whom I was only now getting to know. There were able journalists like the red-headed Donald Thornton from

Arbroath and his wife, Helen Fisher, daughter of a former
Broad Street character, Pat Fisher; there were breezy young men
like Kenneth Peters and Bob Smith and sages like George
Fraser and the lonesome Cuthbert Graham who, when you
could penetrate his painful shyness, would fascinate with tales
of his friendship with Lewis Grassic Gibbon and how they had
driven south together on that occasion in 1934 after Gibbon's
very last visit to the North-East, the handwritten manuscript of
Grey Granite now in his pocket for a final revision before going
to the publisher. When I met him in his mid-forties, Cuthbert
Graham was little known to the public, apparently happy to
remain a studious backroom boy of journalism which suited the
physical handicap of a badly crippled leg. But his vast knowledge of North-East history, its castles and its folklore, gradually built him a reputation through the sixties and seventies,
when he charted them all in the weekend review of *The Press
and Journal*. Like all the best developments, his stature grew
slowly but it was well rooted and bound to blossom in time. In
an age of vanity, when pomposity seems to score over real
worth, how splendid that a man as modest as Cuthbert Graham
should finally be dug out of his cocoon and marched high upon
a dais at the University of Aberdeen to be publicly declared an
Honorary Doctor of Laws.

So Cuthbert was there but some of the other personalities
had gone, notably George Rowntree Harvey, who was not only
a fine poet and playwright but widely regarded as one of the
finest critics of music and drama in all Britain. Like many
another journalistic genius, Rowntree Harvey had a fondness
for the bottle and during my early days in Turriff I had
watched, fascinated, as he slept through an entire performance
of *The Messiah* in St Ninian's Kirk – and then produced a
brilliantly-constructed criticism in the following morning's
issue of *The Press and Journal*. When you remembered that he
had seen *The Messiah* eighty-five times it was less surprising
that he found consolation in a good dram and an even better
sleep. George Rowntree Harvey belonged to that breed of
Bohemian bachelor, bow-tied and theatrical, warm, wayward

and untidy, a home-bred Aberdonian with cosmopolitan over-
tones who was equally at home in obscure conversation with
learned professors and in unpatronising patter with the clean-
ing wifies at *The Press and Journal* office. He was the brilliant
wit and mimic who became the inspiration of a lively student
life at the University of Aberdeen immediately after the First
World War. George Fraser told me later how Rowntree Harvey
had attended university by day and worked full-time as a sub-
editor by night, never asking for a single evening off, not even
for the final examinations which were to bring him a first-class
honours degree. His name was soon legendary far beyond his
native land and when it came to his funeral at Kaimhill Crema-
torium, the amazing breadth of his circle was truly reflected in
the assorted gathering of human beings.

Among the missing faces when I returned to Aberdeen from
the Buchan office was that of Ian Howard, a quiet, lanky lad
who had come north from the tenements of Glasgow to learn his
journalism in the calmer pastures of *The Banffshire Journal*
before transferring his genius as a lay-out expert to the *Evening
Express*. Ian and I had shared an attic room at an hotel in Albyn
Terrace and generally engaged in adventures both journalistic
and otherwise. One night Ian vowed that he could lure the
highly popular Beverley Sisters, who were appearing in town,
from under the chaperoning eye of their father. It was regarded
as an impossible feat but these were a speciality of the persuasive Howard. The fact that we ended that evening with the
Beverleys on our knees, driving along the Prom in an old
Morris car driven by George Chrystal (better known as cartoon-
ist Chrys, the creator of Wee Alickie) is more than just a
pleasant memory. It told me something about the quiet determination of Ian Howard which was to make him one of the
most significant journalists of his day.

He had long since returned to his native Glasgow to make his
mark on the *Scottish Daily Express* when I received a message
one January day in 1960 that he wanted to see me immediately
in the City Bar, across from *The Press and Journal*. He was
asking me to join him as a sub-editor at the *Daily Express* in

Glasgow at a salary of £25 a week, which seemed like a fortune in 1960. I was earning £16 a week in Broad Street at a time, before inflation, when salaries of £25 belonged to another bracket. What's more, a job on the *Express* was the envy of almost every journalist in that era. It was the paper with flair and excitement, created by men like Lord Beaverbrook and his famous editor Arthur Christiansen. The reign of Christiansen in London had run parallel for twenty-five years with that of Sandy Trotter as editor of the *Scottish Daily Express*, the sister paper, but both were now drawing to a close. A fiery Sassenach called Roger Wood had taken over as editor in Scotland and one of his first tasks was to build up a depleted sub-editing staff, thus the instruction to Ian Howard to find new blood. His first step was to the familiar territory of Aberdeen where he sought to recruit Duncan Macrae and myself.

Four years earlier I had married Eden Keith, whose father was headmaster at Strichen, and she required no persuading that we were on our way to Glasgow, perhaps en route to Fleet Street. I left Aberdeen Journals in the time-honoured fashion of a drunken presentation, filled not only with whisky but with an enthusiasm for the wider world, yet harbouring a mild regret that I would not be savouring the full flavour of a Broad Street tradition which had stretched from the John Sleighs to the Rowntree Harveys, the Andrew Ingrams, the Cuthbert Grahams. Where again would I find such men? Where would I find a caseroom with such intellectual giants as George Dunn? (It says a great deal for the Thomson Organisation that they spotted the talent of that humble craftsman and eventually made him managing director of their publishing centre at Withy Grove, Manchester.)

On Leap Year Night of 1960, having travelled down on the train from Aberdeen, I mounted the stairway of Lord Beaverbrook's glass palace in Albion Street, Glasgow, to present myself as a sub-editor of news stories, an area of 'subbing' where I had very little experience. Secretly I was hoping that I could pick it up quietly before they decided I was not worth my new-found wealth!

The editorial floor of the *Express* was a large, open-plan system so different from Aberdeen, where reporters and sub-editors had worked on separate floors and even in small compartments. Here was a free-ranging hive of activity, buzzing with the kind of vitality which seemed to typify the spirit of Glasgow itself. Shirt-sleeved executives on the news desk conducted a kind of frenetic performance of news gathering which owed at least something to Hollywood and must have done more for the adrenalin than it did for the nervous system. Along another side of the vast area, sports phones were ringing and confusion was reduced to a semblance of order by a splendid man called Bruce Swadel, who wore formidable boots and looked less like a sports editor than a baillie dysting down the byre to muck the nowt. At least that reminded me of home and so did the voice of the chief sub-editor, Ronnie Sangster, whose father was a butcher in Aberdeen.

Across the editorial floor the familiar faces of the day would flit. John Mackenzie was called the 'Voice of Football', blossoming in stature with the kind of confidence which the *Express* could instil in its writers; Kevin Fitzgerald was known as 'Scotia', the best racing tipster in the land; Magnus Magnusson would drift over from the features department, sporting an image which was much less staid than that which turned up in his later days as a television pundit. But the hub of a national newpaper is the sub-editor's department where the whole assorted mass of news, sport and features is drawn together and shaped and chiselled into the final production of next day's newspaper. It was around that horse-shoe formation that I settled myself on a February night in 1960, feeling my way quietly into the atmosphere of the great *Daily Express* on a nightly routine which ran mainly from 6 p.m. till 2 a.m., with a canteen break at 9 o' clock.

It was a bustling, tiring, smoke-filled night which hovered forever between excitement and hysteria as editions were either caught or missed. A murder trial in Glasgow would mingle with a Free Kirk row in Skye, a beauty queen elopement in Dundee and the fish prices from Peterhead. And when the frenzy of the night's production had died down we would put on our coats and step out into the smoggy air of industrial Glasgow, sometimes walking all the way home in the hope of clearing the head of smoke and noise and restoring a normal blood pressure before going to bed.

Such was the reputation of Glasgow in those days that I chose to walk home only if there were two or three of us going in the same direction for our route to the South Side took us through the Gorbals, where close-mouths were worth a careful glance in the passing, or so it seemed. By chance I had found myself a bungalow in Burnside, which still reeked of the mass murderer Peter Manuel, for it was here that he had so recently massacred the Watt family on his way to becoming Scotland's most notorious killer of all time. Oddly enough I had seen Manuel in Peterhead Prison in the early fifties when he was serving a sentence for a previous rape. But I paid less attention to him than to people like Johnny Ramensky, the notorious safe-blower who interrupted half a lifetime in Peterhead with a distinguished wartime career when he was parachuted behind enemy lines to use his delicate expertise in the blowing of safes and the stealing of vital documents.

While the feeling was still fresh, I absorbed the true essence of Glasgow through the filter of my senses – Glasgow, that great conglomeration of villages, city of golden hearts and stainless steel razors that guarantees to kill you, with kindness if not with cutlass, city of tongue and twang where even the church organs are liable to have glottal stops. To this great parish pump, far from the fresh fields of Buchan, I took my ploughman's stride, a motion which starts somewhere in the marrow of the bone, and there I ploughed an uncertain furrow through streetfuls of ricketty, bow-legged men and fat, asthmatic women, gravel-voiced beer-barrels and pint-sized nyuchs who would raise hell in the name of the Pope or King Billy yet never enter a church or think of religion as anything but a noble pretext for a 'square go'.

As nights wore on, I applied myself diligently to the fashioning of other people's writing, feeling that the raw copy of the

Express reporter fell short of the standards on *The Press and Journal* and *Evening Express*. So I would re-write it to my own idea of clarity and extend that principle to the *Sunday Express* for whom I worked on a Saturday night. I thought I was doing no more than an average sub-editor should; but here again, the standards of an Aberdeen training stood me on good ground. I was asked to become Chief Sub-editor of the *Sunday Express*, on top of my daily duties and I ran a dual role through the middle sixties.

But there is a limit to the satisfaction of polishing other people's prose and soon I was submitting the occasional article to the features department and finding myself with a by-line on the pages of the *Scottish Daily Express*. One day I noticed the features boss, a blunt but breezy Dundonian called Drew Rennie, pacing up and down near my desk. It was much later I discovered that he was trying to pluck up courage to ask if I would write an article based on a news story of that day. The story was about a soldier being court-martialled for desertion and the explanation in his defence was that he had a bad stammer and fellow-soldiers were making his life such a misery that he could stand it no longer. What were the agonies of having a stammer? Since the verbal banana-skins had plagued me since early childhood I was well qualified and perfectly willing to write about it, so Drew Rennie could have saved himself the embarrassment. It was at that point that Ian McColl, an outstanding editor of the *Express*, suggested I should make my choice between a sub-editing career and a writing one. I jumped at the latter and embarked upon the most exciting period of my whole life. The bulk of the work as a features writer, I found, was in Britain but every so often there was a trip abroad, fitting in with my ambition to see the world. So, in a sense, the *Express* became a vehicle on which to fulfil some personal ambitions.

I had no sooner come under the brilliant leadership of Drew Rennie than he told me one December morning in 1964 to get myself to Italy as quickly as possible and to make contact with Helenio Herrera, boss of Inter Milan and the greatest football coach in the world. Glasgow Rangers had been drawn against his team in the European Cup and, in a familiar *Express* tradition, we would want to 'ghost' a series of articles about Herrera and his views on Rangers, Scotland and football in general. It was my first professional experience of grabbing a passport and some currency and catching a plane to a foreign country at short notice. Inter Milan were playing Fiorentina on the Sunday so I flew via London to Rome, drove once round the Colosseum in the airport bus and caught a train to Florence.

Herrera was the biggest name of his day in world football and just how powerful a figure in Italy I was soon to discover. Without a word of Italian I had difficulty in finding where he and his team were staying for the match with Fiorentina. Finally a taxi-driver took me on a run into the country and deposited me in pitch darkness at a mansion where, he understood, the Inter Milan party were staying. It turned out to be the Villa la Massa, a fifteenth century castle converted into a hotel, and there I verified the presence of Herrera and booked myself in. Having been surveyed with curiosity, I was further baffled in the baronial dining-room that night to find that there was one long table for the Inter Milan party and a small table for me, without another soul in sight. When Herrera's men boarded their bus for the match next day, the entire staff of the hotel were packing their bags to leave as well. Then it was explained to me that Villa la Massa was a seasonal hotel which opened for one night of winter, recalling its staff for the sole purpose of accommodating Herrera and his national heroes. My attempts to sign him up for an *Express* series, which included an invitation to visit Glasgow, were met with a command to appear at his home in Appiano Gentile, north of Milan, on the Monday morning. As a dictator in football, his authoritative manner tended to spill over to private conversation.

I duly appeared on his doorstep on a dull, foggy December morning and negotiated a deal in a form of pidgin English which left me wondering if I had unwittingly committed the *Express* to paying a fortune. Among the lessons I had learned in those three days were how to find your way about a foreign country when you don't know the language, and what to expect from a razor-sharp brain in a business transaction. I also learned that I could go all the way to Italy with a lucrative contract for Mr Herrera – and he didn't even ask me over the doorstep for a cup of tea or glass of vino or whatever they drink in Milan. They would have had better manners in Maud!

The involvement of Rangers in another European football match – the Cup Winners' Cup Final in Barcelona – set me off on a mission to Moscow to see how the other half lived, the supporters of Moscow Dynamo who would not be able to join the 20,000 Rangers fans at the Spanish stadium. Anxious days of pleading and persuasion at the Soviet Embassy in London (and some personal advice from Sir Alec Douglas-Home) produced a last-minute visa and I was on my way to Moscow, via Copenhagen, in a big Ilyushin plane.

The flight into Soviet territory began with the chilling instruction over the intercom to put away your binoculars. Once more without the language, I was busily engaged with the phrase-book to ensure that at least I knew the difference between 'da' and 'niet'. When I found that the Russians put 'c' when the sound is 's' and 'p' when they really mean 'r' then I gave up trying to understand their hieroglyphics and ordered myself a double vodka. The only piece of verbiage which seemed to make sense was the word for brassiere, which is pronounced 'lift-chick', and that at least proved that the Russians are not without a sense of humour!

When the Ilyushin touched down at Moscow Airport and unloaded its luggage, the Russians were covered with embarrassment that they had mislaid my travelling bag in Copenhagen. While they sorted out who was due for a long stay in Siberia, I sauntered out to the taxi rank, minus razor, toothbrush, pyjamas or a clean shirt, and hired a car to take me to the flat of a journalist in Kutuzovsky Prospekt. That was when the Russians lost track of me. Firmly seated in the back of a Communist cab, I absorbed my first impressions of life in the Soviet system. By the light of early evening women were still toiling in

143

the fields as we passed that memorial point where the invading German armies of the Second World War were finally turned back to perish in the freeze of a foreign field.

I spent the next few days at large in the Russian capital, taking in the breadth and beauty of that impressive city and finding out about how the people live. It was a unique opportunity, enriched by the help of a splendid interpreter whom I managed to engage for the duration of my visit. Through her I was able to meet scores of people and to learn about their life-style as they went about their daily routines. At the end of the working day it seemed that regimented hordes would all flock in one direction to the large departmental store known as GUM, near Red Square, before flocking off again towards the Underground warrens which would lead them home. I found that, when Ivan had reached the large block of flats which was home to most people and had consumed his beetroot soup and sliced sausage, the chances were that he would turn his thoughts to football.

Outside the Dynamo Stadium I met large groups of supporters just standing there, like cloth-capped Scots of the thirties, discussing the merits of last week's match and the prospects for the one to come. When they discovered where I came from, they gathered round to give my interpreter the busiest hour of her life. She was intrigued to be in the middle of such a frank exchange of views, so clearly a rare experience in a Communist country. My attempts at finding out about them were more than balanced by their own attempts to learn about life outside the Soviet Union. Their ignorance of basic facts was quite pathetic and what a pleasure it was to enlighten them, even a little, about the way we live. They were delightful people, eager for knowledge and friendship (and perhaps freedom) and it was sad to think that such a minor encounter had been like a major event in their lives. But heavy-jowled men appeared on the fringe of our gathering and for the future safety of my interpreter I bade my Russian friends farewell and beat a hasty retreat. Their parting handshakes and smiles and wistful looks still haunt me to this day. I watched them in greater mass at the

Lenin Stadium, where the Central Army was playing Kiev Dynamo and found that football supporters behave much the same the world over. Any notion that Ivan on the terracing is a dour comrade in long coat and dumb emotions can come only from the imagination of a movie-maker. As they bawled abuse at the referee it came clear to me that this was perhaps their only opportunity to kick against authority without risk of a train-ride to Siberia.

This was a Moscow where no one could own his own house, where they joined long queues for food – and where they still took out your appendix with a local anaesthetic. Surprisingly, it was a Moscow with a serious beer-drinking problem, a fact which was confirmed as I left the Lenin Stadium that evening. No alcohol was permitted inside the football ground but they made up for it at the beer stands on the approach roads where the gutters were lined with drunks, left to sober up in their own good time, I was told.

A journalist friend put me right on the private enterprise ventures which manage to survive in Moscow. For example, if I were waiting for a bus and an unmarked car drew up and offered me a lift, it would be quite safe to accept. I would merely give the driver a rouble (about fifty pence at that time) and he would take me anywhere in Moscow. He would simply be a worker driving a State-owned car across town and taking the chance of some pocket money en route. Sure enough, it happened as the man said, convincing me that capitalism is not dead in the Soviet Union.

Back in Red Square, where no traffic is permitted, the crowds paid homage by the portrait of Lenin and the golden domes of the Kremlin shone out a reminder of another age. Earlier in the day I had walked through the walled enclosure of the governmental seat with a keen awareness of the dictatorial oppression. Now five illuminated ruby stars stood out as an impressive contrast to the night sky and, from the dining-room of the National Hotel, which looks across Revolution Square towards the Kremlin, I surveyed it all with a deep sense of the history. So much had happened in that astonishing country in the 800 years since the Kremlin *was* Moscow.

In a city which was geared up that night for the visit of President Nixon, there was an air of anticipation at the National Hotel as Russian families joined gaily in an evening of food and good fellowship. A bell rang out across the moonlit city and the little orchestra struck up 'Midnight in Moscow'. Another day had ended in the Soviet Union. Tomorrow it would be time for the homeward journey, my notebook filled with interviews and impressions. I had met such men as Lev Yashin, Russia's World Cup goalkeeper who was coaching Dynamo under the direction of another football legend, Konstantin Beskov, remembered as the dashing inside-left of the famous Dynamo team which played Rangers in a memorable game in 1945.

When I arrived at the airport for the journey back to Scotland, via Paris and London, I was suddenly confronted by grim-faced officials who bundled me into a cell-like interrogation room and demanded to know where I had been. I should have been staying at the official tourist hotel and they had lost all trace of me. Well that was their bad luck. I had had a marvellous time in Moscow. What's more, my bag had now turned up so I would be able to shave and wear a clean shirt. With bad grace, they finally escorted me out along a red carpet and drove me to a waiting plane, through massed ranks of Soviet soldiers and military bands. I thought they were really over-doing the ceremonial – until I remembered that, as I flew out, President Nixon flew in!

Back home, the career of Ian Howard, the man who took me to the *Express* in the first place, had rocketed to high success before disintegrating into a series of disasters in his private life. He had been to America and back when he phoned me one day from a Glasgow hospital to ask if I would visit him. His marriage was broken, he had few friends left and he had just suffered his sixth heart attack. Ian Howard should just have been approaching the prime of a brilliant career but the bloated wreckage I found at the hospital that night was merely struggling to stay alive. Recollection of our early days in Aberdeen produced the boyish laughter I had known so well and we spent a happy hour together. My plans to help in his rehabilitation were superfluous, however. Ian died a few days later.

Chapter Eighteen

On Board the Queen Mary

The three familiar funnels of the old *Queen Mary* rose above the dockland clutter of Southampton Harbour as my taxi headed towards the greatest ship that ever sailed the seas. I was on my way to America for the very first time with plans to interview people like Richard Rodgers, composer of some of our greatest musical shows, and Lester Pearson, Prime Minister of Canada. The visit was partly professional and partly private but it was really sparked off by the news that Malcolm Forbes, son of Bertie, was planning a sumptuous celebration to mark the fiftieth anniversary of *Forbes Magazine*. I had vowed all those years ago that I would become a writer – and that I would attend one of the big whingdings at *Forbes*. It had been too far for my parents and grandparents when they were invited by Bertie himself but there would never be a better occasion than the Golden Jubilee dinner. I was turning it into the central feature of a prolonged stay in the United States, at which I would represent the corner of Scotland where the whole romantic story of Bertie Forbes began. What's more, I was going to do it in style. While there was still an ocean liner to float you over the Atlantic there was really only one way to travel on your first visit to America. Compared to the six-hour flight in an airliner the five-and-a-half day voyage to New York was just about right for a gradual adjustment to the cultural shock.

So there I was, about to board the *Queen Mary* on her third last trip before she was sold off by Cunard to take up some static position at Long Beach, California. Stepping out of the taxi, I stood in disbelief at the size and scope of that magnificent lady, her black outline soaring to the heavens and dwarfing all around her. Slowly I made my way up the gangplank and disappeared into a different world – a floating island of fun and fascination, of good companionship and the most gracious living. In the gathering excitement of impending departure, people found their cabins, explored the vast avenues of the ship and gathered on deck as the crowds on the quayside waved and cheered. At the end of an era they would not see this sight too often again. As the tug-boats guided us down the channel towards the open sea, the burning torch of Fawley oil refinery lit up the night sky then faded into a distant spark as Britain sailed out of our reach and we entered the dark and lonely acres of the ocean.

To walk inside the *Queen Mary* was like entering the largest and most luxurious hotel in the world, where there was so much to do and absolutely no obligation to do it. You could walk up spacious staircases, surveyed by the portrait of *Queen Mary* herself, flit from games deck to the cinema or the swimming pool or simply drift from the Verandah Grill to the Midship Bar, strolling, jogging, dancing, drinking, talking, according to the mood of the moment.

But the centre-piece of that magnificent ship was the main lounge, more elegant than any hotel I had seen, high-pillared and wood-panelled with an air of majesty which summoned up an age that was gone. Amid the tinkle of afternoon teacups, leisured ladies did their crosswords with only a gentle grind of vibration to remind them that they were somewhere in mid-Atlantic and not in Mayfair. On a flower-decked stage where Henry Hall was once the maestro, a small string orchestra of bow-tied gentlemen was gliding into the honey-toned melodies which lent the final touch of Palm Court atmosphere to a scene of pleasant anachronism.

In the gathering momentum of night-time the revelry became fast and furious, music filtering from every deck and echoing across the churn of the Atlantic Ocean. Day by day the air grew warmer till the crew changed into white tunics and you sensed the gradual approach of the New World. In the moonlit cool of late evening I would walk out on deck and survey the splendid isolation of our ship at sea, appreciating the soothing therapy of simply taking your time on the way to America. (What an eerie business it was on the Sabbath of our crossing to hear the church bell peeling out across the parish of the Atlantic.) Back inside, the bars were filled with people exchanging stories of where they came from and why they were going to the States. Everyone had a story, whether it was a British couple going to visit their exiled relatives, a shrill American lady who had just done Europe, or an idle roue, complete with gin and tonic, who had been on this ship so often that he couldn't remember if he was coming or going. Having stood with Captain Treasure Jones on the bridge of the great ship, I then accepted an invitation to his cocktail party, a semi-formal occasion which more than lived up to its reputation. At meal times you kept to the same table where eight or ten of you were liable to form a lasting friendship. And so it was on that auspicious voyage when my companions included Professor and Mrs Harry Barth from New York, a delightful couple with whom I still correspond.

The last night on board ship is always a gala occasion. After dinner Mrs Barth persuaded me to join in the last session of bingo, a pastime which I had strenuously resisted till then. We arrived in time to collect the very last card in the very last game. Such was my ignorance of this idiotic pursuit that Mrs Barth had to instruct me on the most basic of rules. When I had run through all the shouted numbers she propelled me to my feet to call 'Bingo!' I felt ever such a fool as I was ushered to the dais by a red-coated gent amid a flourish of musical chords. However, I felt less of a fool when he announced that I had won the week's accumulated jackpot of 160 dollars. That was my first and last game of bingo and it heralded such a night of champagne as to put us in poor shape for a clear-headed arrival in New York.

Nevertheless, by 5 a.m. we were all on deck with a bleary-eyed sense of anticipation, wrapped up in sweaters as the first cold light from the east revealed a shadowy land-mass ahead of us. Distant lights began to twinkle out of the dawn and a cigar-smoking American drawled the information that these were the lights of South Brooklyn, yeah man. Closer and closer it came with the rising light when, out of the haze, grew the Verrazano Bridge, the longest suspension in the world, bearing its early morning traffic on the way to work. It was just another Tuesday as the great *Queen Mary* slid under its girders. The sudden appearance of the Statue of Liberty to the left brought us clustering to port side. Then just as suddenly we headed for the bows as the mighty skyline of Manhattan peered through the morning mist and rooted us to the spot like mesmerised rabbits as we silently beheld one of the legendary sights of the world. We just stood there with our own thoughts, striving to fit the reality into the framework of a long-established image and allowing the magnetism of Manhattan to pull us close to her warm and welcoming breast. Even when you are near to the lower end of the island and the skyscrapers are clear and close, what strikes you most from the estuary is the utter silence of the noisiest city in the world.

It was H.G. Wells who said that the view of New York from a distance was not so much that of a city but of a collection of boxes from which a city might be unwrapped. Well, as the *Queen Mary* finally edged into her berth on the Hudson River, New York unwrapped itself all right, the teeming noise of the city suddenly breaking over you like a tidal wave in a cacophony of dockside din, hooters blaring, porters shouting and yellow cabs screeching to a halt. The farewells taken, the baggage gathered, I turned for a last look at the Grand Old Lady of the Sea and hailed a taxi which drove me down Broadway and along 42nd Street to the Tudor Hotel, which was close to the *Daily News* building, where the *Daily Express* had its office.

The Forbes celebration was several weeks away so I settled myself in with the *Express* staff and went out to explore this intriguing island which the Dutch originally bought from the Mana-Hatta Indians for a few ribbons, beads and trinkets worth twenty-four dollars. They called it New Amsterdam but the British captured it from the Dutch and it became New

York. Then the Americans captured it from the British and it became neurotic. Some dismiss it as a concrete jungle but New York is a wonderfully vibrant, exciting city, dramatic in its broad avenues running down the island and its gently undulating streets running across it. I steeped myself in the atmosphere, walking, talking, exploring and absorbing till I was totally ensnared by her alluring charms. Just to stand in Park Avenue, outside the Waldorf Astoria Hotel, and to consider that the glass mountains around and above you are man-made is one of the bewildering experiences of a lifetime.

My first interview in America was with one of those legendary figures whose name and music had reverberated around the world so long and so powerfully that it was hard to imagine him as a recognisable human being. To meet Richard Rodgers I took a lift to the fourth floor of an office block in Madison Avenue where I was shown into a well-appointed suite, hung with framed mementoes, a typical business office in midtown Manhattan except for the grand piano which stood out as a clue in the corner. The muted noise of traffic rising from the street below was the nearest thing to the sound of music I could hear as we settled down to talk across a desk. Could the small, dapper, unimpressive figure really be Richard Rodgers, composer of as great a wealth of popular melodies as one man has ever produced? It was hard to fit someone so unassumingly ordinary in appearance into the legend which his talent had created, yet it taught me the lesson that greatness burns quietly in the heart or soul or mind of a human being without regard to the wrapping. I turned it all over in my mind as we talked – the memorable pre-war partnership of Rodgers and Hart which was followed, on the death of Lorenz Hart, by an even greater partnership of Rodgers and Hammerstein. That second period alone had given the world an array of musical plays which ranged from *Oklahoma* and *Carousel* to *South Pacific*, *The King and I* and *The Sound of Music*. Richard Rodgers looked every inch a business man, adding to the picture by travelling to his office most days from either of his homes in Manhattan or Fairfield, Connecticut.

I found Rodgers a difficult man to interview. For someone who had cascaded with beautiful melodies for half a century he seemed strangely short of emotional content. His answers were clipped and measured and precisely to the point and he insisted that his output had nothing to do with inspiration. He merely wrote according to order, providing appropriate musical sounds for the mood of the story presented to him. I still refuse to believe it but this was how Rodgers himself explained it to me:

'I am not the kind of composer who wakens up in the middle of the night with an idea and springs out of bed to put it down on paper. I have to sit down and concentrate – and work. It begins with the idea of the play, the situation and the character. If I have a lyric I can go ahead and write the music. Sometimes I do the music first but the important thing is the situation and the character. And that is usually provided by someone else . . .'

The 'someone else' who inspired the melodic genius of Richard Rodgers to reach its heights was, successively, Lorenz Hart and Oscar Hammerstein, the men who wrote the words. Both were gone by then and, since Hammerstein's death in 1960, Rodgers had written *No Strings* which was a success in America, and *Do I Hear a Waltz?* which was a failure. He never did find a third partner, nor was that surprising since he had already had the good fortune to attract two of the greatest lyricists of all time.

Richard Rodgers, son of a New York doctor, had amassed a fortune which at that moment was being expanded by the cinema success of *The Sound of Music*. He was astounded to hear that it was still running in the same Glasgow cinema after two years and nine months and that encouraged him to speak warmly of his visit to Scotland in 1930 for the opening of *Evergreen*. Gradually it became clear that the cool manner was simply the nature of a genuine and modest man – and that the measured speech may well have another explanation. I braced myself to ask the delicate question at a time when cancer was even more of a forbidden subject than it is now.

'Yes, it is true that I have had cancer. I have not kept it a secret,' he told me. 'It was in the jaw. But that was twelve years ago and I was cured. I had a check-up for it yesterday and I'm all right.'

I thanked him for revealing so much of the character and humour of the American people. In plays like *Oklahoma* I could instantly recognise the country folk of a land I had never seen as being the same country folk of my own native corner.

I told him that the wind which swept down the plains of Oklahoma blew just as surely in the far corners of rural Aberdeenshire where my own mother went about her housework on the farm, whistling a happy tune which could originate in a Manhattan skyscraper but struck a universal chord in Maud, Milan and Melbourne. Through an unchanging expression I knew that he was deeply moved by the tribute. As we shook hands I knew too that I was leaving a lonesome man, one who had taken us through a chorus of tunefulness from *Blue Moon* to that last song which he and Oscar Hammerstein sat down to write together, *Edelweiss*. His consolation was that his music was capable of cheering so many millions of people. His last words to me were: 'Yes, I would like my music to live.' And who can doubt that it will?

As I flew north from Chicago to keep an appointment in Ottawa with Lester Pearson, the Prime Minister of Canada, all eyes were on the main headline of the day – the downfall of the previous Prime Minister, John Diefenbaker. Not only had he been voted out in favour of Pearson but he had now been kicked out as leader of his own Conservative Party. The big showdown had just taken place at the party convention in the Maple Leaf, Toronto, and this was surely the end for Dief. There was a note of regret all round for, even if his career had gone sour, Diefenbaker was still regarded as one of the greatest Canadians of the century. I changed planes at Toronto Airport and hurried across the tarmac to take up the last remaining seat in an extra flight to Ottawa. Having fastened my seat-belt, breathless from the rush, I sought to regain my composure in the silence around me. Once more all heads were deep in the newspapers. 'Dief the Chief – it's the End' they said. Casually, I glanced across the narrow passageway and who was sitting next to me but Diefenbaker himself, gazing into space with the heavy eyes of private grief, his wife Olive resting a consoling hand on his arm. The Press had been pursuing him at Toronto and they would be waiting for him again at the Canadian capital but here I had him to myself, practically sitting on my lap! Was it prudent to intrude on his privacy at that moment? Should I try to interview him there and then? I decided to await our arrival in Ottawa, spending my time observing at close quarters the emotions of a great Prime Minister in this hour of personal defeat. I smiled respectfully and kept close on his heels as we left the plane and crossed the tarmac to a waiting battery of Press and television men.

The Press corps of Ottawa were obviously in a sympathetic mood as he paused to give his obligatory few minutes of general interview.

'What do you plan to do now, Mr Diefenbaker?' asked one reporter.

'Well, I guess I'll go out West and do a bit of fishin',' he replied.

As he answered further innocuous questions it struck me that, in his moment of uselessness, he would relish the opportunity to get his teeth into something positive.

'Mr Diefenbaker,' I began. 'As a visiting journalist from Great Britain, can I ask if you have anything to say to the people of the Old Country in this, your moment of departure?'

The big issue of the moment was that appalling speech by President de Gaulle in which he had called out to his French-Canadian audience '*Vive le Quebec libre!*' It was a mischievous call for a split in the nation.

John Diefenbaker turned slowly and said: 'Yes. Yes, I do have something to say to the people of Great Britain.' Cameras whirred, pencils hovered over notebooks. 'I want the people of

Britain to know that, even if I am no longer at the centre of Canadian politics I shall fight till the end of my life to preserve a one-nation Canada.' And from there he launched into a major speech, short but snappy, which gave the old warrior an escape from his grief. There was spirit in him yet and when he finally stepped into his limousine to be driven away, hard-bitten journalists put down their gear and gave him a spontaneous round of applause. He rolled down the window and said: 'Gentlemen, you don't know how much that means to me.' Tears were streaming down his cheeks. What a poignant moment in Canada's political life I had just witnessed. Since I had sparked it off, the journalists crowded round to thank me for putting in the vital question. That night it went out across the nation on radio and television. Next morning I had an appointment with Diefenbaker's successor, the very different personality of Lester Pearson.

After a night at the magnificent Chateau Laurier Hotel in the Canadian capital (Ottawa has something of the atmosphere of Edinburgh) I walked to Parliament Hill and was guided along a corridor to the Premier's office. Lester Bowles Pearson was the fourteenth Prime Minister of Canada, variously regarded as informal, friendly, complicated and a master of dignified protocol. Moreover, he had taken on a kind of balancing role between Britain and the United States. As an international figure of significance he was playing host to the world which had come to join in the massive world exhibition known as Expo 67. All this coincided with the centenary of Confederation for Canada as well as with his own seventieth birthday.

But if ever I needed a lesson that great men are really very ordinary mortals at heart it came to me in Lester Pearson's office. For there he sat, with the pin-striped appearance of a local lawyer, drinking coffee out of a blue and white mug that you would find on any working man's table. He swivelled in his big leather chair and began to question me about my late boss, that remarkable Scots-Canadian Max Aitken, better known as Lord Beaverbrook. I took my cue from Russia's Jacob Malik who once said: 'I always listen when Lester Pearson speaks', and we got on like a house on fire. The former history professor talked historically of how Canada had lived under the shadow of Downing Street in the early days and latterly of America.

'Our way of life became North American and, in some ways, quite indistinguishable from the United States, except in Quebec,' he said. 'Now we realise in this centennial year that it is a great thing to be a Canadian and we have learned for the first time how to celebrate Canadianism with a kind of nationalistic fervor. One of the reasons why we have suspected patriotic breast-beating in the past may have been that the Scottish element is so strong. By tradition the Scots don't go in for that. Their emotions run deep and do not readily show. So we were more reserved and there was a stability and dignity of life. But this has changed and I believe it is for the better.'

In the wake of the de Gaulle speech we were able to talk about the problems of the two-language nation and a wide variety of other subjects. One of the pleasures of interviewing the really top people in life is that there is practically no question which cannot be asked. They will give you an answer of some sort.

Pearson drank his coffee as we looked out towards the Mounties parading before Parliament Buildings. Visiting heads of state were there for the Canadian celebrations and a tap on the door reminded him that he was running behind time. Mr Pearson apologised for the hustle and, as I was shown out, the President of Italy was shown in. Another busy day was under way in the Canadian capital. The work of a nation awaited.

The strength of that Scottish influence which the Prime Minister had mentioned was all around in evidence. Indeed is there a family in Scotland today without a branch in Canada? In my own case the Canadian relatives now outnumber the Scots with the majority in the Toronto area. In the familiar fashion it happened around 1910 that Uncle Jimmy Barron, a brother of my grandfather, set out from the North-East with his wife and ten children for a new life in a new world. Prospects for country folk in Scotland in those far-off days must have seemed as bleak as the Hills of Fisherie, making the very name of Canada sound like a romantic escape from drudgery. So they sailed away from

Greenock, out across the bare Atlantic on such a rough and miserable voyage that they vowed they would never set foot on a ship again – and they never did. From the St Lawrence they had to find their way to Guelph, Ontario, where a small farm awaited their attention. When they got there, I am told, Uncle Jimmy put down his case, surveyed the new abode with a scratch of his head and said very little. His children casting anxious eyes on their father could only guess at the thoughts running through his head.

Nearly sixty years later I was now walking up that same farm road to meet Uncle Jimmy's children, by then in an age range from 58 to 80, and putting myself in the boots of that Buchan man arriving there in 1910 with all those children and responsibilities. I could have a fair guess at those thoughts which were passing through his head. Roughly speaking, he must have been questioning the sanity of coming all those thousands of miles for this. Canada, a land of opportunity, ready to flow with milk and honey? That small-holding on the plains of Ontario looked just like a thousand other bare bit places on the grudging clay lands of Buchan. But with a stomach and an equilibrium sorely turned upside down by that nightmare voyage, the destiny of Jimmy Barron and his wife and ten children was there in Guelph, for better or worse.

And there they settled down and made the best of it, in all truth not much better than they would have done at home. His remains had gone to dust long by now but bachelor sons still farmed the same land and the others were clustered around the area. True to the vows of 1910 not one of those elderly Barrons had ever set foot on a ship – nor a plane for that matter – to see their mother country and my arrival was a matter of great curiosity and even celebration for I was the very first relative from Scotland they had seen in all those years.

What a marvellous moment it was as I approached them outside the farmhouse where they had all been children together. All except one of the ten were there, lining up as a kind of guard-of-honour, and there I was, walking up the line shaking hands with people I could have picked out of a multitude as being blood relatives of my own. Mary was just Auntie Annie all over again. John Barron was just another version of his namesake cousin back home.

Inside, the kitchen was just like an old-fashioned kitchie on a Buchan farm, made all the more quaint by a stove in the middle of the room with the lum going up through the ceiling. Having known I was coming they had baked a cake, suitably inscribed, and their children and their children's children gathered round and we had a fair old party. Outby in the fields they seemed to scrape a living which could never have brought them riches. And in one corner of the barn lay an old-fashioned trunk with the initials M.B. It was one of the kists which had brought their worldly belongings on that journey from Scotland. Such was the pattern of immigration. In this simple way the Scots had been taking their families and their skills to foreign lands for hundreds of years. You marvelled at their sense of adventure and indeed that very quality, allied to their energy and desire to create a better life for themselves, must surely explain the prosperity which came to so many of their adopted lands.

When the acquaintances had been soundly forged, the greetings and memories exchanged and the food and the drams well and truly consumed, I was on my way to further travels in North America. As I headed for the trouble city of Detroit with its streets aflame in the race riots of 1967, the Barron family were still there at the door which had given them a childhood home all those years ago. The umbilical cord of a family stretches across oceans, a fact which came clear to me as I turned and waved and felt the sharp sting of a lump in my throat.

So I journeyed on through the North American continent, sampling their motels and their hamburger stalls and attuning my heathery lugs to a language which seemed to have a recurring rota of words and phrases like 'Huh', 'Right', 'You're welcome' and 'It's bin nice talkin' to you.' There were Bar BQs and even Car BQs (were they selling cars or turning them on a spit?) and there was a gradual acceptance of the American people for what they are. And what are they? They are a serious-minded, hard-working and hospitable people so blessed with both the energy and naivety of youth that they never know when they are beaten, so they never are. They may create a farce like their early attempts at launching a rocket from Cape Canaveral but they pursued the problem – as they do with all their problems – until they finally beat the Russians in the race to the moon.

An obsession with health means that everyone knows his calorie intake; an obsession with education means that everyone seems to have graduated from one college or another though, in all truth, their basic instruction falls far short of what we learned at Maud School. Nevertheless the American talks with a freedom and confidence which makes him sound a great deal more educated than he is. A Buchan loon might know a damned sight more but he won't say it half as well! The travels and the interviews and the general intake of the American life were building up to the grand climax of my main purpose in coming to this great land in the first place.

As a preliminary to the gigantic party which would celebrate the fiftieth anniversary of *Forbes Magazine* I walked down Fifth Avenue, central artery of Manhattan island and one of the most impressive streets in the world. There is Tiffany's and the Empire State Building and a mixture of people and cultures, sights and sounds, yellow cabs screeching, lights which say 'Walk' – 'Don't Walk', feathered flunkeys, dull-eyed junkies, high-stepping ladies, low-shuffling beggars, the famous, the forgotten, the has-beens and the never-weres, all contained in the kaleidoscope of human flotsam which makes up New York. Down Fifth Avenue towards Greenwich Village my eyes settled upon a building which set my heart beating just that little bit faster. Above the flutter of the Stars and Stripes the name was emblazoned for all to see: *Forbes Magazine*, headquarters of an organisation which owed its very existence to a lad from a country cottage in Aberdeenshire.

Bertie Forbes was gone but his creation lived on, housed in a building of neo-classical charm and character which was formerly the headquarters of the Macmillan Publishing

Company. Macmillan's had built it, they said, from the profits of H. G. Wells' *Outline of History* and Wells himself was among the visitors, along with Sean O'Casey, James Mitchener, Kathleen Windsor and Margaret Mitchell, the creator of *Gone with the Wind*. It was here that a brash young editor asked Kathleen Windsor if *Forever Amber* was based on her own bedroom experiences. 'No' replied Miss Windsor. 'If it were, I never would have had time to write it.' It was a building of marble staircases and chandeliers while next door stood a magnificent town house which Bertie's son Malcolm used for the entertaining of distinguished guests.

Malcolm's own home, however, lay across the Hudson River and out into the rural peace of a New Jersey estate called Timberfield. On the big night I was driven out to the Forbes home in a gleaming limousine, along with Bertie's loyal secretary, Gertrude Weiner, and his niece from Glasgow, Agnes Baird. Security officers vetted the arrivals at the gateway while inside, private airplanes were touching down on a specially-laid airstrip, bringing four hundred of America's business and political leaders and their wives to what was generally acclaimed as the biggest spree that that great nation had seen for a generation. Every president or chairman, from Coca Cola to General Motors, was there filing through the Forbes mansion for a personal introduction to the guest-of-honour, the Vice-President of the United States, Hubert Humphrey.

Thereafter we sauntered out to the lawn for cocktails in the warm air of a September evening, the ladies attired in the very best that America's richest men could buy. But darkness came early to the peace of the Timberfield valley which dipped below the lawn and as cocktail glasses clinked and moguls dangled at the end of outsized cigars there came a sight which startled even the most blasé out of their cynicism. Suddenly the gathering dusk became a glitter of floodlights and across the valley from the trees beyond came a hundred pipers playing *Scotland the Brave*. Lips which spell out million-dollar deals fell apart as those giants of Wall Street took in the incredible spectacle and confessed that, while they had seen just about everything in this goddam life, they had never seen anything quite like this. Hell man, this sure was something. Up they came to the manicured lawns, this parade of exiled pipers, a rousing echo of dear auld Scotland, forming a guard-of-honour for the guests as they trooped into the massive marquee where the anniversary dinner was being held. It is a well-worn joke about everything being bigger and better in America but the joke is on those who don't believe it. All the superlatives could not do justice to the fabulous events of that evening which began with the mellow strings of a massive orchestra performing on a stage bedecked with a plane-load of heather flown in from Prestwick.

We ate and danced and drank far into the night, Hubert Humphrey and I sharing a joke that we were the only two people there who were not Presidents! More chillingly, and in the light of recent events in Dallas, Texas, he could have been said to be just one shot away from being President of the United States. But this was a night for warm celebration in which Humphrey made a memorable speech, paying tribute to Bertie Forbes, the boy from the Cunnyknowe who took the standards of an Aberdeenshire cottage and used them as the yardstick by which he judged the shadier sections of business behaviour in his adopted land. Thus he became known as 'the great humanizer of American business', honoured by universities and respected all the way from the cottar houses of Buchan to the White House of Washington. It was a long way from New Deer to New York but that was the journey which little Bertie Forbes had taken so many years ago. He had encouraged me into journalism and here I was, amid the music and champagne and general euphoria of a special night in American history, rubbing shoulders with the mighty and reflecting on a scene which could not have been further removed from the origins of that romantic story.

It was indeed a far cry from the plains of Buchan as I turned it all over in my mind on the journey back to Manhattan. Dawn was already breaking over the skyscrapers of New York as the Cadillac delivered me in full evening dress to my hotel in 42nd Street. With the time difference, they would already be half-way through a morning's yokin' in the hairst fields of Buchan, with little thought or caring for a fancy spree in a far-off land. Yet, to the extent that this had been Bertie's night, it was their night too. At the centre of the top table that evening had been Malcolm Forbes, carrying on the tradition of his famous father, just as he carries on to this day the magazine column which Bertie made popular on Wall Street and which is headed with a text he took from his days in the family pew at New Deer: 'With all thy getting, get understanding.'

Chapter Nineteen

Chasing Charlie Chaplin

From the Atlantic to the Pacific I had seen that great American continent in the turmoil of a social revolution which ranged from the black uprisings of Detroit to the drug-assisted love-ins of the Flower People by the Golden Gate Park of San Francisco.

Back home in Britain the Rock 'n' Roll explosion of the fifties, which had blown sky-high the reigning standards of restraint and discipline, had given way to a more sophisticated social order which was generally described as the 'Swinging Sixties'. It was a stimulating decade, made all the more so in my own case by the range of people I came to meet. Even before that spell in America I had come in contact with a man who was to become the best-known name in the world, Cassius Clay, later choosing to call himself Mohammed Ali. He had already set the boxing world alight with his destruction of Sonny Liston and everyone was talking about this phenomenal fighter.

My encounter with Ali came about because I had some experience of the art of ghost-writing. That simply means you interview someone then write the article in the first person as if they had done it themselves. There is nothing dishonest about it. You are merely absorbing their thoughts and feelings and putting it all down as they would wish to express it. The first book I ever wrote was a 'ghosting' job, the autobiography of the immortal Jimmy Johnstone of Celtic, a football genius whose talents would never have extended to writing his own book. So I did it for him and the formula has become commonplace in modern times, especially among sports books.

The *Express* had signed up Mohammed Ali for a series of first-person articles during his visit to Britain and I became the ghost-writer, travelling with him, eating with him, staying close enough to see and hear what was happening yet keeping discreetly in the shadows at the proper moments. With his regular flow of language Ali was, of course, a ghost-writer's dream, pausing from time to time to rattle off the kind of phrases which were unmistakably his own. In his build-up for an exhibition fight at the Paisley Ice Rink he travelled around like the celebrity he already was, meeting a bewildered public, signing autographs and generally playing the role for which he was to become even more famous.

His interest in verse prompted a visit to Burns's Cottage at Ayr and as we browsed round the little, white-washed house, Ali marvelled at the poetic creations which had sprung from such a humble base. He drew his hand over the bed clothes, turned the spinning wheel and fell into an unaccustomed silence from which he emerged to say: 'Man, I was feeling 'way 'way back in time just there. It does you good to pause sometimes and think about these things.'

The highlight of his day came when he sat in Burns's own chair, made out of the printing press which turned out his early editions. The Muse was not long in alighting on his broad shoulders for soon the Heavyweight Champion of the World was starting to reel off those verses which, even then, were coming to him so naturally. They came in odd scraps like:

> Now this man Burns lived far out of town
> It wasn't always easy to get around
> He began to find he'd plenty of time
> So he sat right down and started to rhyme. . . .

Then he was entertaining a growing band of admirers with frivolous stuff:

> I've heard of a man named Burns

– supposed to be a poet
But if he was, how come I didn't know it?
They told me his work was very very neat
So I replied: 'But who did he ever beat?'

It was all carried out in a spirit of great good humour. But the most touching moment of my time with Mohammed Ali came at the MacDonald Hotel, on the south side of Glasgow, where he and Sugar Ray Robinson and most of the American boxers have chosen to stay down the years.

We were sitting at lunch one day when a little black nurse appeared at the dining-room door, shyly indicating that she wanted to speak to Ali. She was being given precious little encouragement until Ali sensed the situation and beckoned her in. The little lady introduced herself as Jen and recalled that she was one of the kids he used to play with in their backstreet days in the state of Ohio. Of course! He remembered her well. So a chair was pulled up and Jen was invited to join us for lunch as the two of them delved back into their childhood days in less affluent surroundings.

It transpired that Jen was training as a nurse in Glasgow, still at the bottom end of her profession, when she announced to her superintendent that she knew Cassius Clay – and that she would ask him to come and visit the children in the Western General. There had evidently been explosions of disbelief and amusement at the claims of this little Miss Nobody. How could she possibly know the Heavyweight Champion of the World and how would he ever agree to interrupt his busy schedule even if she did? Well, can you imagine the scene as Mohammed Ali and I showed Jen into our classy limousine and drove up to the superintendent's office? Yes, yes, it was all true. Jen was indeed his childhood friend and he was delighted to come and visit the sick children in *her* hospital.

When Jen's superiors had managed to close their gaping mouths and rub the disbelief from their eyes, they led the Heavyweight Champion on a round of the wards where he played games, signed plaster-casts and kept up a non-stop patter which delighted his young audience. In the midst of it all he pulled me aside and said: 'This is the sort of thing ah like to do for ma people. Just think what this will do for little Jen.' There was no doubt that her achievements of that day had given her a new status. Her superiors were looking on her already with fresh respect and I always cherished the thought that the confidence which blossomed before our very eyes was the starting point for a successful career in a noble profession.

Wherever he went in Glasgow, into shops, banks or walking on pavements, traffic came to a halt and there was minor pandemonium. He accompanied me to the *Express* office and took over the daily editorial conference from Ian McColl, the editor. Then he would withdraw to his hotel room and dial Los Angeles for it was the mid-sixties and there were race riots in the Watts district of the city, in which he showed a keen interest.

Street riots in America seemed a far cry from the more orderly ways of Britain at that moment but I was soon to learn that we should be careful about smug comparisons. Before long, the *Daily Express* was running a headline which said: 'Express men caught in gas attack'. Imagine the horror of my father and mother in Maud as they read that their only loon had struggled to a telephone, suffering from a bellyful of the Army's notorious C.S. gas, to report the news that all hell had broken loose in Belfast, with gun battles, bomb explosions and the dead and injured lying everywhere. It was early days in the modern upheaval of the Ulster people but that particular night was to become known as the most violent in fifty years of Irish troubles. When the dust had settled and I had cleared my lungs of that fearful gas, I gathered my thoughts to write an article for the Express, from which this is an excerpt:

By the time I got to bed on Saturday, five people lay dead – two of them snipers gunned down by the Army – and dozens more, including 19 soldiers, were injured. All this in a land whose coastline at its nearest is just 13 miles from Scotland.

The first essential in a situation like Belfast is to sort out the niceties of noise, the crack of gunfire from the light boom of the gas grenade and the heavy thud of a bomb explosion. We had them all.

Then you learn the geography of the city in terms of the Catholic and Protestant areas, and the history in terms of the Unionists, Republicans or Nationalists and their multifarious offshoots.

Beyond that, there is the constant interpreting of events – why the stones, the barricades, the burning buses? Until you get to grips with the Irish position at close quarters the bald events can be oddly meaningless.

The weekend stones began to fly because the troops went in search of guns in the houses of Balkan Street. In one of the houses lay the corpse of a teenage girl and the menfolk didn't like it. That was when we began to dodge a hail of bricks and bottles.

The soldiers countered with C.S. gas and that was the moment when I did not require a second telling to beat it, running left and right in a blind agony of burning eyes and choking throat.

A kindly old lady called out 'Here me boy, dip your hanky in this and soak your face.' I did and found enough relief to see that most other people were in the same predicament. That antidote to C.S. gas was vinegar, supplied in bowl or bucket on window sills for everyone's use.

As the troops withdrew, a bulldozer came roaring round the corner with a scoopful of bricks, dumping loads at every street-end. The people of the Lower Falls were storing up their ammunition, some of it paving stones dug up with a pneumatic drill in readiness for a night of trouble.

They hi-jacked local buses and pushed them across the entrances to their symmetrical little streets to keep out possible attack from Protestants.

I found myself behind these barriers and soon up against a wall being closely questioned by a group of vigilante youths as to why I was there. Scottish journalists were not high on the popularity list and the situation looked ugly before I was finally cleared of suspicion. Some were for 'taking him inside' and I could only plead that I was a personal acquaintance of Jock Stein, whose respected name was plastered high on a facing wall.

And with darkness came the bullets, a full-scale shoot-out between the British troops and the stray gunmen of Albert Street, Servia Street, Leeson Street.

Down came the curfew in which everyone was ordered indoors except for a brief outing to collect milk and essential supplies. The people were allowed out again to church and Curfew Town came suddenly alive. The nightmare of bullets and bombs was over, for the moment at least. Now it was time to dress up in their Sunday best for Mass.

Children came out to play with the Army sandbags, finding some consolation for their weekend of bewilderment. Older folks said they could not remember anything like it, even in the 1920s. At lunchtime hundreds of Catholic women, singing cheerfully, came marching down the Falls Road from other districts with loaves of bread and bottles of milk to hand to their friends and relatives inside the curfew area.

Meanwhile the soldiers counted up the haul of captured arms – 52 pistols, 35 rifles, six automatic weapons, 100 incendiary bombs, 25 pounds of explosives and 20,730 rounds of ammunition, enough to supply a battalion.

In the midst of a Belfast battle scene the incomer does not stop to question the insanity. He accepts it at face value – and runs like hell.

That was just the start of my encounters in trouble-torn Ulster as I proceeded to dodge the bombs and bullets on many a frightening night. Perhaps the most hair-raising took place in the Turf Lodge district of Belfast when I was travelling with an Army patrol inside an armoured car (known as a pig). The rattling of dustbin lids was the way of spreading the news that the Army was here and we were soon under ambush from a hostile crowd who finally exploded a nail bomb beneath where I was seated. The tragedy of Northern Ireland has continued to plague us in an age of scientific wonders when mankind has come to expect that there must be a solution to every human problem. Whatever expedients may be found by the politicians, I would offer the depressing postscript that the troubles of the Emerald Isle may prove to be without any real solution at all.

On a lighter note, there was another insoluble problem of that period: trying to interview Charlie Chaplin. I had been trying repeatedly to make contact with the great actor, intending to visit him at his home in Vevey, Switzerland. But protective secretaries merely confirmed what was already well-known about Chaplin – that ever since those McCarthy days in America, when he was the subject of a witch-hunt for his allegedly Left Wing views, he would have nothing to do with Press interviews.

After five-and-a-half years of pursuit I was ready to give up, believing that there was a limit to the endurance of the most persistent of journalists. Then I heard that Chaplin and his wife Oona, daughter of the famous writer, Eugene O'Neill, were to take a holiday in this country, his first visit to Scotland in fifty years. It was too good a chance to miss. Somehow I had to find him and talk to him. My only clue to his whereabouts was a rumour that he would spend a night at the Tor-na-Coille Hotel, Banchory, but the receptionist there had been suitably briefed to keep the matter private. I knew by her reaction, however, that he was definitely coming so I booked myself a room and prepared to wait until Chaplin arrived. I then posted myself in the reception area, casually drinking cocktails and coffee and with one eye on a book and the other on the door. I did not have too long to wait. On my second day at the hotel a sleek limousine drew up at the doorway of the Tor-na-Coille and out stepped the greatest cinema legend of all time, a stocky little man of eighty-one, a raincoat hanging unbuttoned and a soft hat on top of his white hair.

I kept my distance, observing the check-in procedure, the disappearance to a private suite and the re-emergence at the cocktail bar, where the Chaplins chatted happily with mine host, Matthew Armstrong, and other guests. I dined at the next table that evening and sat fascinated by the gestures and mannerisms of a man who still bore the unmistakable trace of his great days on the screen. He still tilted his head in that bashful way of making an overture to a lady, in this case his beloved Oona, his fourth wife by whom he had eight children and with whom he had found his deepest serenity.

It was not until later that evening when he had gone upstairs that I made my introductions to Oona, explaining the innocence of my purpose – simply to talk to the great Chaplin and then write about him in the most affectionate way. The days of witch-hunts were surely gone and would he not accept at face value a Scottish journalist whose motives were strictly honourable?

Oona understood and promised to put the proposition to her husband, though she explained that he was extremely tired. She would bring his reply in the morning. I was already in position in the foyer when the Chaplins came for breakfast but her news was depressing. Regretfully, Charlie would not break his rule about interviews and there was no more she could do; she was sorry. I thanked her and knew that, as they prepared to leave after breakfast on the next stage of their holiday, my one and only opportunity in a lifetime to make contact was slipping away. There was just one chance left. I had brought along my copy of Chaplin's book, one of the finest autobiographies ever written. Would he sit down and autograph it while Oona went back to gather their bags?

He agreed and I helped him into a low sofa from which his aging bones might feel less inclined to emerge as soon as the signing was over! As he wrote – and to my astonishment – he began to answer my questions about the life which had taken him from poverty in the East End of London to great fame and fortune as the king of comedy. Was there a child in the world who did not regard Charlie Chaplin as a friend?

He had known every famous figure from Caruso, Valentino and Rachmaninov to Churchill, Einstein and H.G. Wells. We talked . . . and he sat . . . and we talked. At one stage I noticed that his nose had begun to run and he searched in vain for a handkerchief. Quickly I produced a clean one and he wiped his nose with that old familiar twitch. I asked him to keep it but he insisted in handing it back and we played out a short comedy routine reminiscent of his old films. 'Nowadays I live in Switzerland,' he said, 'and Oona and I go on holiday to Africa. But this year I said "Let's go to Scotland." Now we are heading towards Aberdeen and the south.'

Aberdeen? How would he like to see the old Tivoli Theatre where he had performed in the early years of this century? That familiar smile broke over his face. Yes, he would rather like to see the place again. Well, I would lead his chauffeur from Banchory to Guild Street for a brief stop before he headed south. It was all fixed. I made frantic contact with *Daily Express* photographer Ron Taylor who would record the precious moment at the Tivoli.

And so it happened. The chauffeur-driven Daimler drew up at the Tivoli door and out stepped the legendary Chaplin to pause with his memories of sixty-five years earlier. The entrance still beckoned you to 'Fauteuils and stalls' but now the show inside was bingo, not music hall. 'I used to come here both before and during my Fred Karno days,' he told me. 'In fact I was only about fourteen or fifteen at the time. I came to Scotland with "Sherlock Holmes" and we played here and in smaller towns like Dumfries and Dunfermline. I had a clear impression of Aberdeen and I did so want to see it again,' he added. And he marvelled at the beauty of what he had managed to see.

By now word had spread that Charlie Chaplin was here and within minutes a crowd had materialised. 'Good old Charlie', they called. As he glanced from side to side I half expected to see the little tramp accelerate round the corner, tripping the pursuing mob one by one with the crook of his stick. Instead he smiled, patted heads, signed autographs and realised in a heart-warming moment that there was a whole new generation of kids in this age of television to whom he meant just as much as he had done to their fathers and grandfathers. We took our farewells and I conveyed him back to his Daimler.

It had been a memorable episode and now he was seated in the back beside Oona, the woman who took his attention, as he said himself, 'with a luminous beauty, sequestered charm and gentleness'. Together they drove off, smiling and waving to the large crowd. I knew then the legend of Charlie Chaplin would never die. And that, having brought me the rarity of an interview with the man himself, my patience over five-and-a-half years had been well and truly rewarded.

The Chaplin experience taught me a lesson in perseverance which served me well in a similar pursuit of the richest man in the world, Paul Getty. Time after time I had sought an interview with Getty at his magnificent residence of Sutton Place, the stately home in Surrey which he had bought from the Duke of Sutherland. Getty, of course, was an American domiciled in Britain and owing his massive fortune to an uncanny nose for oil. His millions outstripped even those of the mysterious Howard Hughes.

Such men are generally hard to pin down and harder still to question about the secrets of their wealth so it came as no surprise when I was regularly passed on to a gentleman called Mr Wallace, who was never blunt enough to close the door completely but was always advising another call in about a month's time.

Patiently I followed the instruction, not just for two or three months but for EIGHTEEN of them! On that eighteenth call I asked as usual for my Mr Wallace and the girl on the Sutton Place switchboard plugged me into an extension. When the voice answered I said, as always: 'Is that Mr Wallace?' 'Mr Wallace?' queried the husky voice at the other end of the line. 'No, you've got the wrong extension. This is Mr Getty speaking.' 'Mr Getty?' I exploded in disbelief. 'Oh, it's really you I want to speak to, Mr Getty. As a matter of fact I've been trying to speak to you for the past eighteen months but I can never get past Mr Wallace. You're always too busy.'

I explained my journalistic mission, with particular reference to North Sea oil, in which Getty had a mere £100 million investment, and he replied: 'And you have been trying to talk to me for eighteen months? Well just you call back Mr Wallace and tell him to give you the first available appointment in my book.'

With a fluster of thanks I rang off and re-called the same number (for once in my lifetime blessing the error of a switchboard operator) and asked for Mr Wallace. As he began the familiar routine of calling back in a month's time I was able to say, with the greatest of authority: 'Mr Wallace, I am not asking for an appointment this time. I'm telling you! On Mr Getty's instructions, find me the first available appointment.'

'Mr Getty's instructions?'

It did not take long to convince him that I had spoken to the man himself – and within a week I was driving out into the Surrey countryside in a taxi and presenting myself at the first hurdle of security for the richest man in the world. Any notion that money means freedom takes on a farcical aspect when you find yourself passing through a system of electronic gates and being cautioned by a guard that you cannot walk in these grounds alone for fear of being savaged by the dogs. They snarled from every enclosure along the way to the mansion which was set within a massive acreage. To gain some impression of the scale of Getty's home you had to consider, for example, that the front lawn was fifteen times the size of Hampden Park. The rest of his life was built to match.

By a chain of aides I was conducted through this sumptuous mansion, which was built by Henry VIII for one of his knights, until we finally reached a rather modest-looking den where I was left alone with Jean Paul Getty. The picture was rather a pathetic one. For the man who counted his millions by the hundred was sitting alone with his shoe and sock off, nursing an agonising foot which all the money in the world could do little to ease. He apologised for the indignity of the situation but soon adjusted his mind to the matter of North Sea oil and began to answer my questions with a measured judgment which gradually revealed the tremendous depth of the man.

Greatness comes in a variety of guises but Getty seemed to feed your questions into a computer where a vast mechanism of knowledge, experience, instinct and wisdom produced a print-out which told you clearly that there is no substitute for the supremacy of human genius. He himself had bought up plot after plot which spurted oil with remarkable regularity. In 1949 he drew forecasts of bankruptcy when he bought the rights to a stretch of the Arabian desert which seemed like an endless waste of barren sand. In fact it turned out to be one of the most valuable oil properties in the world. Getty had a natural instinct for oil and helped me to put the North Sea saga into perspective by illustrating that there was a single oilwell in the Middle East which had more reserves than the whole of our Scottish waters put together.

It was springtime in the English countryside and together we looked out upon acres of daffodils as he contemplated a life which had been filled with the tragedies which so often beset the rich. His eldest son George died of an overdose of drink and drugs. The young son of his fifth marriage, whom he adored, took a brain tumour and died when he was twelve. There had been family rifts and finally there was the kidnapping of a grandson whose ear was chopped off.

Paul Getty, a man of deep culture, turned slowly to me with a wistful look in his eye and said: 'But I am an optimist. You have to be. There is no room for pessimists in the oil business.'

He bade me a courteous goodbye and invited me to come again. I turned on leaving the room and found him waving a frail old hand. The richest man in the world was not just alone but lonely.

I had come to know people like Bing Crosby to the point of exchanging Christmas cards and found the Old Groaner by far the easiest man in the world to interview. Once again it was a case of penetrating the barrier of protectors, often self-appointed, to find that the man himself was as free and amenable as one could wish for. Meetings with Crosby became as regular as they were delightful. He would tell me stories of the great American composers who were a particular interest of mine – the Gershwins, Berlins, Kerns and Porters. Having recently spoken to Irving Berlin and marvelling that he was writing popular songs in 1906 and was still doing so more than sixty years later, I appreciated one of Bing's tales in particular.

Irving Berlin made a point of keeping the copyright of everything he did, which showed that his business sense was as sound as his melodic inventiveness. Bing told me about the big musical they were making in Hollywood, featuring Berlin's music. In one particular song they needed to change key in the middle, a modulation which required the insertion of one single note. But it wasn't as simple as that. The director had to call in Berlin's lawyer to explain the situation. There was deep discussion and furrowed brows till the lawyer finally agreed to get on the phone to Mr Berlin in New York. Having fully explained the situation he waited for the master's permission to insert that vital note. There was evidently a long pause while the composer pondered the copyright position. Then he permitted himself a slow and cautious reply. 'Yeah,' he said. 'Yeah, I suppose that will be all right. But remember – it's MA note!'

Chapter Twenty

Hitler's Friend – and Mine

Adolf Hitler and I had one thing in common –a mutual friend whose name was hardly known to the general public but who must rank as the most intriguing of all the people I have ever interviewed.

In the bid to play down the Hitler era after the Second World War, the German people had conveniently forgotten that Dr Ernst Hanfstaengl ever existed. But I had heard of him and managed to track him down at his villa in an exclusive suburb of Munich where he had lived for most of his extraordinary career as Press Chief of the Nazi Party and close friend and counsellor of Hitler, with a totally unique insight into the character of that fiendish man. It was Putzi Hanfstaengl (that was his popular name), the semi-aristocrat of big, broad build and charm to match, who took Hitler from the beer-halls of Munich and introduced him to the culture of the Hanfstaengl home, where the politicians, artists, writers and other influential people had a habit of gathering.

It was Hanfstaengl, himself taught by a pupil of Liszt, who became Hitler's favourite pianist, summoned from his home by car on many a night to play lullabies for the Fuhrer when he couldn't sleep, which was often. It was Hanfstaengl who brought Hitler and Churchill to within a few yards of each other in a Munich hotel before the Nazi leader chickened out of an encounter which might have done wonders for world history. It was Hanfstaengl who came to know so much about the sexual deficiencies of the shrill little monster who had long pestered Mrs Helene Hanfstaengl (daughter of a German-

American business man) with his amorous attentions. Finally it was Hanfstaengl who fell foul of his leader in 1937, escaped an attempt to assassinate him and fled to Britain where he was interned at the start of the Second World War. During the war he was transferred to the United States and became adviser to his old Harvard Club friend, President Roosevelt, on political and psychological warfare against Hitler.

The stories of this colourful career, verified by several of the Nazi war criminals, became a special fascination to be savoured over a period when I was a regular visitor at his charming home in Munich, the same house where he had entertained the Nazi hierarchy and where he would point out that Hitler used to sit there and Eva Braun there, and Goering and Goebbels over there, during their vigorous days of the twenties.

There we would talk into the night in a dimly-lit studio-room, piled high with musty books and magazines, still laden with an atmosphere of power and lingering evil – and finally enriched by the music which flowed from his old grand piano as he sat himself down on Mozart's own piano stool and ran his masterful fingers along the keyboard.

On one of our last evenings, when we had decanted an impressive array of wine bottles, he was full of nostalgia for an America which had given him not only his mother but firm friendships with people such as Roosevelt, William Randolph Hearst, T.S. Eliot and Walter Lippmann. He had, in fact, just returned from the 65th anniversary reunion of his Harvard classmates. His original arrival at Harvard in 1905, at the age of eighteen, had brought him to a country familiar not only because of his mother but because the family business of art reproduction had by then a branch on New York's Fifth Avenue.

His college days over, he stayed on to look after the branch, suffering the sticks and stones of anti-German feeling during the First World War. By 1921 the call of the Fatherland took him home to a Munich already embroiled in the ominous rumblings of Communism and other political agitations. Then one day he had a phone call from Warren Robbins, another ex-

Harvard contact who worked at the American Embassy in Berlin, to say that he was sending down an attache to assess the on-goings in Bavaria and he wanted Hanfstaengl to introduce him to the right people. The attache arrived – Truman-Smith was his name, a Yale man but not a bad fellow for all that – and spent a few days summing up the situation before returning to take his leave of Hanfstaengl. 'I met the most remarkable fellow I've ever come across this morning,' he said. 'Adolf Hitler is his name.'

Hanfstaengl, who knew everyone worth knowing in Munich, looked blank.

'Are you sure you don't mean Hilpert, the German Nationalist?' he queried. No no, it was Hitler; and he was to be holding a meeting in a beer-hall that evening for which there were placards saying 'No entry for Jews.' Truman-Smith had to return to Berlin but he wanted Herr Hanfstaengl to attend the meeting and report his impressions to the American Embassy.

So he went along to the Kindlkeller beer-hall that evening, asked someone to point out this fellow Hitler – and suddenly clapped eyes on the unknown figure who would one day change the course of civilisation. Evidently Hitler gave a well-reasoned speech, with all the mark of a great orator and Hanfstaengl told me how he had gone up to the platform at the end to introduce himself. Hitler grasped at the chance of an entry to the Hanfstaengl home with its social graces and valuable contacts. Being himself ill-acquainted with the world outside Germany, he would come to rely on Hanfstaengl for guidance in that and many other respects. He wanted to know about America. He admired the Ku Klux Klan and Henry Ford (because of his allegedly anti-Semitic tendencies and also because he might be a source of funds).

Putzi Hanfstaengl used to play him stirring American marches from the days when he was taken along with the Harvard football team to rouse them to action before a game. He composed some himself. 'That's what we need for the movement,' said Hitler; and in his old age Hanfstaengl would cringe at the thought that it was one of his own compositions which was played by the Brownshirt columns as they marched through the Brandenburg Gate on the day that Hitler took power in Germany.

So the connection grew, at meetings in the Cafe Neumaier or back at Hitler's dull little room at 41 Thierschstrasse, with its threadbare rugs where he would pad around in braces and no collar, and where his collection of books ranged from *A History of the Great War* to the *History of Erotic Art*. He disliked Bach and Mozart but was always delighted when Putzi would sit down and play him the prelude to Wagner's *Meistersinger*. Gradually Putzi Hanfstaengl was able to unravel the mystery of Hitler's sex life and to come up with the intriguing and probably accurate theory about the connection between his hysterical oratory and his sexual deficiencies. The beautiful Mrs Hanfstaengl, who had had to fend off his persistent infatuation, told her husband that the Fuhrer was in fact a neuter, neither fully homosexual nor heterosexual and suffering complexes from the time he caught syphilis in Vienna in 1908.

To Hanfstaengl his speeches were akin to the work of a great orchestral conductor. But he once wrote this interesting observation: 'It was gradually being borne in on me that Hitler was a narcissus type for whom the crowd represented a substitute medium for the woman he did not seem able to find. Speaking, for him, represented the satisfaction of some depletion urge and to me this made the phenomenon of his oratory more intelligible. The last eight to ten minutes of a speech resembled an orgasm of words.'

Hanfstaengl became the man above most who could say almost anything to Hitler and get away with it. Standing tall and impressive outwith the immediate political circle, he occupied a unique position as friend and counsellor, link man between Hitler and the world's Press, as well as pianist, sparkling conversationalist and high-class court jester. Disdainful of some of the human trash who surrounded the Fuhrer, he raised jealousy and suspicion among them, a special position which he relished. Moreover – and only Putzi could have achieved this – he claimed that he never did join the Nazi Party! He did, however, become deeply involved in such ploys as the notorious Putsch of 1923 and had to flee for his life when it came unstuck. Hitler fled one way (to Hanfstaengl's wife at their country home in Uffing) while Hanfstaengl himself crossed to Austria and visited some of Hitler's relatives in Vienna. These included Hitler's niece, the ill-fated Geli Raubel, whom he took to the opera, not knowing that she would later come to Germany, become the object of Uncle Adolf's amorous approaches and finally commit suicide, an incident which seemed to divert him to an even more resolute course of savage behaviour.

Hanfstaengl crept back to Germany in disguise but Hitler was caught and jailed at Landsberg, where he gathered his thoughts for his book, *Mein Kampf*. On the day he left prison he went straight to the Hanfstaengl house at Pienzenauer Strasse in Munich for a celebration dinner of turkey and the rich Austrian pastry which Hitler loved so much. The inner circle was meeting at the Cafe Heck in Munich's Galleriestrasse – and the course towards eventual power was resumed.

It was in the early 1930s, when Hitler was heading briskly towards his dictatorship, that he came to within a few yards of Churchill, the closest the two men ever came to actually meeting. Hanfstaengl was dining with the Churchill family at the Hotel Continental in Munich, to which he had been asked to bring Hitler along. But the latter made his excuses and Putzi had to go alone. As the dinner conversation wore on, he realised how vital it could be to bring the two men together. He told me: 'I excused myself from the table and went off frantically to reach Hitler by telephone to see if he would change his mind. Lo and behold! There he was in the hotel lobby, in his dirty white overcoat and green hat, taking his farewell of a Dutchman. Here was Hitler in the lobby and Winston Churchill in the restaurant and me in the middle failing, I'm afraid, to convince Hitler of the need to come in for a chat. He was unshaven and, in any case, he had too much to do, he said. So I had to go back and put a good face on it. But what an opportunity lost.'

Putzi Hanfstaengl, a man with an enormous capacity for

living, became more and more distressed at the trend of Hitler's thinking and concerned about the influence of men like Rudolf Hess, who was later to rot out his days in Berlin's Spandau Jail. Hanfstaengl's attempts to moderate the course brought him into conflict with the hell-bent aims of his leader and the crisis had to come.

Sitting in his Munich study one February day in 1937, preparing a speech for the 205th anniversary of George Washington, Hanfstaengl had a call to say that Hitler's pilot was coming to collect him. The mission was to go to Spain to complain to Franco about the lack of facilities for German correspondents covering the Spanish Civil War. It was an unusual errand but he complied. On the flight the pilot, who he happened to know, tipped him the wink that this was an assassination bid. There was no intention of landing in Spain. The Gestapo were on board and Hanfstaengl was to be conveniently 'dropped'. Instead, the pilot obligingly brought the plane down with some engine trouble and enabled Putzi to make his getaway across the Swiss border. It was his fiftieth birthday.

It seemed that Hitler's fury had boiled over at tales of Hanfstaengl's criticism, carried to him by Miss Unity Mitford, the British girl who had hopes of becoming Hitler's wife. So began the exile in Britain and America. Lord Beaverbrook took a special interest in his arrival in Britain for Hanfstaengl had once successfully sued the Beaver for £10,000 in the London High Court over a defamatory item in the William Hickey column of its day. But Ribbentrop, who was German Ambassador in London at the time, advised Hitler to prevent the money from being uplifted because of Beaverbrook's immense influence in political affairs. It would do Germany no good at all. So Putzi had to do without his money and now found himself at the mercy of the British when war broke out in 1939. He was first despatched to Beaverbrook's native land of Canada and then to America and it was ten years before he would see his beloved Germany again. When he did so, he gradually settled to a life as quiet as a man of such large personality and joyous extravagance of living can have.

A Germany so anxious to forget its Hitlerism soon managed to obliterate Hanfstaengl from its memory. But having once unearthed him in his secluded setting I continued to visit him more or less every year, taking my wife and three sons for whom it was a fascinating encounter with the reality which had already found its way to the forefront of their history books at school.

We would stroll through the French windows to the lawn or repair to the den with its grand piano and books and lingering sense of the Nazi hierarchy. There Putzi would sit, recalling it all with the aid of expressive hands, a full crop of hair crowning a noble head, the deep voice alternating with a comic falsetto as the jester jested. He would talk and fill up the wine glasses and put it all to music on that fine old piano. I tried to freeze the moments and absorb Putzi Hanfstaengl as a piece of living history, a likeable rascal in his own right, a vital witness to the character of a madman who wrote the blackest chapter of all in the story of man's inhumanity to man.

Chapter Twenty-One

Foo's Yer Kweets?

It is one of the abiding joys of my life that I have been able to carry the boyhood enthusiasm for journalism right through to middle age. The early gloom about my health has added an edge of appreciation to the experiences of life and encouraged me to wring a maximum of satisfaction from all I do. The excitements of famous people and faraway places have been more than I had any right to expect; but now I was putting it all behind me for the moment and looking again at the place where I began with its steady ways and customs, its particular rhythms and very distinctive form of speech.

Robert Louis Stevenson believed that the local dialects of Scotland would more or less die out in his lifetime. Certainly he was still in early middle-age when he died suddenly in 1894 but even if he had lived a normal span he would still have been mistaken in his judgment. As I have already mentioned, the Doric play which my great-grandfather wrote in the year of Stevenson's death survives into the latter part of the twentieth century. Nearly ninety years after Stevenson I would not dare forecast that the rich, expressive dialect of the North-East will disappear in my lifetime nor in that of my children; and that allowing for the fact that it is under its most serious bombardment of all time from the neutralising effects of television.

But if the language survives it is undeniably in the process of dilution, not so rapidly in the accent as in the substitution of the anglicised word for the dialect one. In the thirties, for example, the day after Monday was Tyesday and two days after that was Fiersday, as surely as your ankles were your 'kweets', the hooping-cough was the 'kink-host' and children learned to count in 'een, twa, three, fower, five, sax, seiven, acht. . . .' You might 'tak a muckle clort o' a deem in yer oxters' and regret it at your leisure but the language on which I was weaned was a colourful expression of human thought, with many a word or phrase so hopelessly irreplaceable by an English equivalent. I knew these words because I had heard them in everyday use among the country folk of my childhood. But I do not use them widely now, except as a recollection, and my vocabulary does not compare with that of my grandfather and my own children's knowledge of Scots words will not match my own; so the inevitable conclusion must be that the words will eventually disappear, except as objects of scholarly study. Stevenson was mistaken only in his time-scale.

Yet those words express something deep and eternal in the character of the people who were bred from them and they are readily recognised when the occasion arises. I cannot recall that any of my friends would have claimed the slightest interest in the works of Burns when we were teenagers. That was exclusively for the decrepit. Yet in 1976 I attended the 150th anniversary dinner of Peterhead Burns Club and there, around the table, proposing toasts and drinking to them and generally acclaiming the genius of a master of Scots language, was an array of kent faces from my own generation, now solid, middle-aged citizens steeped in the glories of a man they would not have acknowledged thirty years earlier.

There is another glimmer of hope. In the lifetime of television drama it has become acceptable to parade the accents of London, Wales and the West Country, Liverpool, Geordieland and even the slovenly English of Glasgow. But somehow the richness of the North-East dialect of Scotland was considered too obscure to be intelligible. That insult to a fine native tongue was finally quashed when that brilliant BBC producer, Pharic MacLaren, decided to televise Lewis Grassic Gibbon's *Sunset Song* and proved that the rhythms of Aberdeenshire could be understood and enjoyed not only across the breadth of Britain but over the entire American continent as well.

It was a significant step, giving rise to more television exposure of Grassic Gibbon's work as well as that of other North-East writers like Jessie Kesson (*The White Bird Passes*) and the Buchan fisherman James Duthie (*Donal and Sally* and *The Drystane Dyker*). Interest broadened and the poetry of people like Flora Garry and the prose of that delightfully unspoiled farm servant David Toulmin took on a fashionable mantle.

Their speech was part of that eternal thread of Scottishness which draws us together as a recognisable people and was the firm foundation of my village childhood, where everything was sound and settled and permanent and you were not disturbed by the constant irritation of change for change's sake. Life was based on a fabric of people whose families had been there for as long as your own and whose inter-relationships were bluntly frank. Nobody rose too far without the decided risk of being forcibly brought back to earth with the traditional Scottish leveller of 'Ah kent yer faither'. My own native village of Maud had produced one of the best British playwrights of this century, Lesley Storm – her father was minister at Maud for thirty-five years – but through all the fame and wealth which she gained with plays like *Black Chiffon* and *Roar Like A Dove* she was never known as anything else but her real name, 'Mabel Cowie, the minister's dother'.

In that setting there was a dogged determination towards hard work and good learning and maybe they knocked the stuffing out of us in a pattern of life which left little room for anything that was not worthwhile. Folk who went gallivanting away on holiday were as little regarded as a man who wore suede shoes or yellow gloves. Sex was all right as long as you didn't enjoy it. My father was capable of hard judgments in his earlier days and the maddening thing was that his verdicts on individual worth so often turned out to be justified in the end. My mother on the other hand would take a more liberal view of life and question the devotion to hard work and sensible attitudes as a worthy cause in its own right. Her romantic dreams beyond the bare boundaries of Buchan would have made her suspect in some quarters but she stirred in me a craving for the brighter lights and exotic excitements of a more glamorous world. Washing off the Imperial Leather soap from her face and sitting down to spread witch-hazel jelly on her chappit fingers she would long for the opportunity to dance through the Vienna Woods to the rousing waltzes of Johann Strauss or Franz Lehar. She had never seen an opera in her life but that did not prevent her from memorising every note of *Cavalleria Rusticana* or *Carmen* or a dozen others through listening to the wireless and she could tell me in plain Buchan tones the merits of *Ave Maria* from the pen of Schubert as opposed to the Bach-Gounod version. She was a disciple of the Russian composer Katchachurian thirty years before the public discovered his name from *The Onedin Line* and she would caper around the living-room to the rousing waltz from his *Masquerade Suite*.

So culture came into our house at 2 Park Crescent more or less by the back door and took its place among the homespun life and language of an otherwise average Buchan family. Sometimes the matter-of-factness of our rural ways would spill over to a coarseness which was less than attractive. I can think of the feet-washing, for example, that strange ritual which preceded a marriage and brought out some of the rougher edges of the North-East character. It was counted as a manly act for a whole gathering of weighty chiels to capture the bridegroom on the eve of his wedding and subject him to a rough-and-tumble in a large zinc tub. If his bride could be lured to the scene then she, too, was manhandled to the ceremony and some rugged chap, with the help of a woman body, would unhook her suspenders (who had heard of tights in those days?) and remove her stockings for the fray. It struck me as a cowardly exercise, alarming enough for the spectating child let alone the poor victims. Any pretence of giving the feet of the betrothed a clean start was usually destroyed by the subsequent extravagance of blackening them all over with boot polish. Many a bridegroom went to the altar with skin that was hard-scrubbed and raw from the last-minute attempts to remove some grimy application. A relative of mine became so distressed by the vulgar display that he grabbed his double-barrelled shotgun and threatened to shoot the lot of them and I must say I had some sympathy with him.

The sickening excitement of those feet-washings in the farm kitchen was matched by another local horror from time to time on a Sunday when a dentist came from Aberdeen to hold surgery on a kitchen chair and friends and neighbours came nervously to have their rotten teeth extracted and to spit volumes of dark blood into a white enamel pail. Dentistry has come a long way when I relate my own experience to children who now undergo the most sophisticated treatment, with high-speed drills and orthodontists to straighten their teeth. In 1938 I was laid flat on my back on the kitchen table by Dr Crombie – yes, a doctor, not a dentist – who proceeded to cover my nose and mouth with the terrors of a chloroform mask and tell me to count sheep. I counted close on a hundred of the damned creatures before finally succumbing to the choking sensation of the mask and for the next half-hour he used a pair of glorified pliers to pull seventeen of my first teeth, during which my mother was cooking the mince and tatties through the scullery door. Such was the level of sophistication in the thirties.

But all things are relative as I thoroughly conceded when Granny Barron gave me proof beyond all doubt that it could have been worse. As a young girl she had had her tonsils removed without any anaesthetic at all. The doctor simply turned up at the Schoolhouse of Whitehill one day and told her to lean back on the settee and open her mouth. Without more ado he put a knife down her throat, cut out one tonsil then gave her time to clear the blood and gather her remaining strength and courage. 'Now we'll do the other one,' he said and the performance began all over again. So there is something to be said for modern medicine and methods after all, even if it has to be recorded that Granny Barron nevertheless lived gloriously on to be ninety-one.

Chapter Twenty-Two

The Hive of Honeyneuk

As I cast back over it now I can still recapture the sense of that childhood and youth which had taken me through the thirties into the Second World War and out of it to a world of atom bombs and austerity, bread units and clothing coupons; but it was drawing to a close with the approach of my twenty-first birthday in 1952.

By then a man I was later to know as Bill Haley was formulating a new sound in music which was to hit the world as Rock 'n' Roll and set off a whole new trend in the public behaviour of human beings. The mood of the thirties had carried over to the post-war era, a little threadbare and erratic in its pace, with the Ruritania of Ivor Novello still maintaining its glorious illusion on the London stage. In Scotland a new race of comedians like Stanley Baxter and Jimmy Logan was emerging to extend the tradition of Tommy Lorne, Harry Gordon, Tommy Morgan, Dave Willis and others. But there was a feeling of suspension as if the whole structure might soon collapse and be replaced by something new; and that happened in the early-to-mid fifties when Bill Haley and Elvis Presley in America and Tommy Steele in Britain threw wide the floodgates of a new and more energetic order. The world had at least come alive again, with whatever mixture of consequences.

Before that youth finally slipped away from me, however, my father was casting his eyes upwards from the council house in the village towards the farm of Honeyneuk, just half-a-mile up the brae on the way to Brucklay. For long he had dreamed of owning his own farm and Honeyneuk in particular, for it sat on a picturesque slope with a windmill and encompassed the whole valley from its front lawn. The boy who had become the mainstay of his mother's smallholding at the age of eight would indeed have arrived at the peak of his ambition if he could lay hands on Honeyneuk which was then, at that moment in 1952, on the market for sale. Two hundred acres of it and some was stony land, they said, which played havoc with your plough-shares. But he had plans for blasting the boulders out of exist-ence and turning it into as fine a farm as there was in the district.

John Webster had been a wage-earner all his life and was not a man of capital, but he did possess those incomparable assets of a sound knowledge of his subject, a reliable character and a determination to succeed; in short, he was a bank manager's dream and that was why he had no difficulty in borrowing the thousands necessary to bid for Honeyneuk. It was not my mother's idea of joy to exchange her village home, where the neighbours dropped in at any old time for a fly-cup and a blether, for the greater solitude of the farmhouse. By nature she was a gregarious creature who thrived on human contact but there was no possible hope of thwarting my father in his treasured ambition. He surveyed the broad acres with a stick and a dog and was in no doubt that this was the place for him. So the bid went in and the farm was his and to Honeyneuk they went and there my mother would turn up the volume of her beloved radiogram, which now augmented the wireless, to give full flavour to Dvorak or Tchaikovsky or Strauss and she would gaze wistfully down the brae towards the village where she had spent her happiest years. In place of the ready neighbour she would spend her time in the company of Albert Ketelbey and the glorious sound of his *Sanctuary of the Heart* or *In a Mon-astery Garden*.

As further consolation she had the company of Nigger, a most extraordinary dog who was half a collie and half a Black Labrador but he was almost wholly a gonner one day in 1949 when my father arrived at a farm on the Red Hill and found the man on the verge of shooting the poor brute. 'Na, na, ye canna dae that,' said my father as Nigger pleaded with his big brown eyes. 'Ah'll tak' the beast hame.' Thus Nigger moved from the edge of death to a fulness of life which can hardly have been surpassed in canine history. He became the Websters' dog, surrounded by affection and proving himself a beast of such uncanny intelligence that my mother swore he was human. On his first Christmas morning he returned from a furtive adventure and produced from the tenderness of his Labrador mouth a little chicken, alive, unmarked and terrified. He laid it on the mat between my father and mother, guarded it with one paw and looked up as if to say: 'It's not much but here is a token of gratitude for saving my life.' We discovered that the bird had come from the hen-run of Ann-Jean Stephen, an elderly spinster not exactly famed for her sociable habits. Dad had the devil's own job to slip the chick back where it belonged before the dire deed was discovered! Nigger moved from the village to the farm with the flitting of 1952 and lived on to the ripe old age of sixteen, constantly repaying his debt with an utter devastation of the rat population at Honeyneuk. When he finally died, poor brute, Dad dug him a decent grave at the garden gate and there his bones lie to this day, marked by a few rough stones of remembrance while his soul must surely rest in that corner of the Hereafter where the good Lord keeps his kennels. I can vouch for the fact that there will be no rats in heaven for as long as Nigger reigns.

Meanwhile, my father had set about the blasting of the Honeyneuk stones though he had scarcely embarked on the task when he was overtaken by the notorious January Gale of 1953, the worst in living memory, when houses were blown apart, people lifted off their feet and carried away and the northern half of Scotland was left bare and devastated. That frightening day of 31 January was to carve its own memorial in the clumps of trees atop the Scottish knolls. They stand even now with slanted posture, like ballerinas wilting with outstretched arms, their leafy cloaks in rags and the power to generate their greenery sadly depleted. Everybody had a story to tell, sometimes an exaggerated one, which would illustrate the force of the fearsome blast but few surpassed the one told by my father, who had been trying to explain to another farmer the strength of the wind which had howled around Honeyneuk. 'Ach, that's naething,' said the other chiel. 'We had sic a force o' wind that oor dog opened his mou' tae bark – and farted.'

Indeed the man's story might well have been true for that same gale took hold of the Honeyneuk steading roof, lifted it off its supports and swept it up, up and away, across the woods of Brucklay estate, which lies adjacent, and we never saw it again. With some help from a relief fund my father put on a better roof, believing it was an ill wind that did nobody some good, with windows brought from the derelict remains of Brucklay Castle to filter God's light and to brighten the winter munchings of the beef cattle which were the mainstay of a farm like Honeyneuk. The basics of a Buchan farm were much as they had been for generations, except that the traditional crop of oats, which gave us our porridge and brose and fed the live-stock, was giving way to barley which could either feed cattle or be sold to the distillers for the commendable cause of making whisky. But the farm life which faced my mother in the fifties was a vastly different business from that of her mother in the earlier part of the century. Almost gone were the hens which had scratched about the farm-close at Mains of Whitehall picking up Nature's protein and turning out eggs with rich red yokes which tasted like eggs. The big combines had moved into the trade by then, mass-producing the eggs from hens in soli-tary confinement, encouraging the birds to grow for an early death with injections of stuff which was said to endanger a man's virility. God preserve us! By then, too, my father had decided that it was better to dispense with the farm cow and to buy milk from a travelling dairyman. An older generation would have turned in its grave but this was what the world called progress and maybe it was and maybe it wasn't. For certain the world was changing at the time of our arrival at Honeyneuk.

Was it then that I severed my ties with a Buchan childhood and youth or was it not until some time later when the telephone rang one Saturday morning in my Glasgow home? However it may sound in cold print, there was nothing callous in the introduction which greeted me as I answered the call from my father. 'Well Jack, fit like?' 'Oh nae bad Dad.' 'Well, mother passed away at nine o'clock ...' Thus a Buchan man will announce the death of his wife to their only child and thus a Buchan loon will discover how swiftly the world can become a duller place to live in. The gaiety of spirit had finally been worn down by the hazards of a crippling and chronic bronchitis, that taste of roosty nails, as she had described, which she wanted to tackle by going down 'wi' a barra and spad tae hae a gweed redd-oot'. As the auctioneer's wife she had answered the phone, taken messages and offered advice to most farming folk in Buchan for she had acquired a sound knowledge of my father's business and was blessed with a clarity of explanation which eluded my father.

If I seek the source of my journalistic interest I need look no further than my mother who was a natural reporter. Long after I had left Buchan she kept me fully informed on local life with a weekly bulletin which was a model of keen observation and brilliant description. People felt the better for talking to her and they did not forget. When we held the funeral service in New Deer Church, where she had first joined as a girl along with my father, they said there had never been a turn-out of folk to match it. Eight hundred flocked from all over Buchan to pack out the downstairs of the kirk and none deserved the tribute better. Her dreams of being a ballet dancer came no nearer than a single visit to a performance of *Coppelia* at His Majesty's Theatre, Aberdeen, but she had enriched her life with the joys of music. If I had failed in my promise to take her to Vienna one day there was some consolation in the fact that I had taken her to meet her operatic heroine, Joan Hammond, when she was staying at the Caledonian Hotel, Aberdeen, as well as Max Jaffa, Reginald Kilby and Jack Byfield who were among her other favourites. Through all the music she had absorbed from the wireless there was one particular piece which emerged as her eventual choice above all others.

'Dvorak's *New World Symphony*' she would tell you. 'I want it played at my funeral. Tell Johnny Walker, the organist.' And so it was. When the time came, Johnny Walker was told and the eight hundred souls who flocked into New Deer Church that cold January day were greeted with the strains of 'Going Home' from the Dvorak symphony. Mam was going home all right, much too soon for one who had enlivened all that she had touched; gone with so much left unsaid by a careless son. In the manner of a country funeral we raised our voices and sang *Crimond*, composed just a few miles away by Jessie Seymour Irvine, who sang in her father's church choir along with my wife's grandfather. Then came that other favourite hymn, 'The Day Thou Gavest, Lord, is Ended', before we proceeded up the main street of New Deer to the kirkyard on the Hill of Culsh, a high point from which you could survey the whole of Buchan. And there we laid her to rest as the minister raised his hand in benediction and the wind blew cold over Culsh's brae. I raised my head and saw in the distance Mains of Whitehill, the small farm where she had been born. Half a mile below us was the village of New Deer, where she had gone to school, and further down the naked plain of Buchan I could see Maud, crisp and clear, where she had spent her married life from 1931 to 1971.

'Lay me against the cemetery dyke so that I'll be sheltered on windy nights,' she used to joke; she was one layer short, as it turned out, and there we left her to the gathering darkness of a winter's night with a wind rising snell by the monument of Culsh and a sore tugging at the conscience about leaving her there alone. I like to think that the January blast was of little consequence in the haven of her journey's end and that the hot sing of a summer's day was the climatic background to a Dvorak symphony which would leap and linger to her eternal pleasure in the auditorium of the golden sunset.

We gathered back at Honeyneuk for a dram and had a sandwich and saw folk we hadn't seen for years; it was a time of happy recollection, of good fellowship in the way that funerals tend to be. People are drawn closer in a greater dependence and an unwillingness to part. The women-folk served tea in the best room where the radiogram and the records still lay and where Mam herself had lain till that very day. Then one by one folk left for home till there were only Dad and myself.

Next day I was to drive away south and the parting was bound to be hazardous for two Buchan men, father and son, whose tradition gives them little practice in the art of communication, especially on tender matters. So we stood in the farm-close, awkward and embarrassed, neither knowing what to say to the other. Emotionally, we had been strangers, my father and I, uneasy with each other's company but now, in the very moment when we had lost our common bond, forced into the contact of two little boys who had suddenly been orphaned. In the platitudes of goodbye, we fell into a silence, standing side by side, then as if jogged by the woman who was gone we acted in one movement and clasped each other by the hand. It was hopelessly out of character, daft-like and bizarre for Buchan men, and I wondered when I had last as much as touched my father's hand for it was not in the nature of the creatures to do so. There we stood without words but not without tears till we had regained our composure and self-respect, for Buchan men do not cry.

Thus I stepped into the car and drove out of the farm-close towards Aberdeen and the south, leaving behind the place of my roots and deepest affections and knowing in my heart that it could never be the same again. The setting of my childhood was there before me in all its familiar landscape but suddenly its meaning and its bare beauty had drained to a deadness, for landscapes and what they mean to us live mainly by the people who inhabit and enrich them. Whoever created the cliche about no one being indispensible must surely have forgotten about mothers.

Well into his sixties, my father was still planning the future of Honeyneuk with a stretch of vision and anticipation which pre-supposed a lengthy stay on this earth. With a keener awareness of life's limits, my mother had poked fun at his sense of immortality and chided him for not drawing in his horns. But

Dad would seldom take a telling. Lack of a father may have given him an early independence but it left him without a checking influence. His enthusiasm for the single-minded pursuit of farming had, indeed, given him a sense of immortality, as Mam had said, but a couple of minor dwams at the mart at Maud were Nature's hint and the next time I was visiting him he casually mentioned that I should carry on the farm 'if onything ever happens tae me'. It was the first time he had acknowledged the possibility, however remote, but his instinct was sure once more. The gradual clogging of a cerebral artery became complete in one day and the life of John Webster, dynamic, good-humoured, quick-tempered Buchan farmer and auctioneer, virtually ended on that Burns' Day of 1976. He never made another decision, though he lingered on for sixteen months of predictable decline until the night in May, 1977, when a further stroke put him into his final hours.

I arrived at Honeyneuk in time to wipe his fevered brow and, as I did so, the black crow of death came settling on the window-sill as an omen of the inevitable. I would not have believed that such things really happen. Whatever he knew or could see or hear or think in those fading hours we shall never know for he was gripped in an involuntary rhythm of heavy breathing, like the bellows which once blew his mother's peat fire into life or out of it. This time there was no choice and I knew that I was about to witness the moment of death for the first time. The bellows-breathing ended and the upturned eyes reverted to a normal setting but the head came forward in a jaw-jutting determination to live. In the very throes of death and with the doggedness which sustained his character, John Webster was not prepared to go without a fight. A last gesture of defiance then death came down over his face like the final curtain of a theatrical production, leaving no doubt that the performance of life was over. John Webster: 1905–1977. So that was how, in the briefness of a few seconds, a human life comes finally to a close. The moment itself seemed unworthy of the wealth of time and experience and effort which had gone before.

THE HIVE OF HONEYNEUK

Outside on a fine Spring night his cattle munched at lush grass on the land which he had made his own, fields which he had cleansed of the inhibiting stone through fifteen years of relentless blasting and turned into rich acres of fertility. A tractor bleated on a distant hill and raucous laughter came through the still air from the village below, loud and uncaring, to prove that life will go on as ever. But at Honeyneuk, the farm which he had longed for those many years ago and had finally acquired and tended and loved with an unspeakable devotion, the maister was at rest for ever. Charlie Fraser, the grieve, came up and so did Jimmy Mutch, the baillie, and tea was brewed for the gathering relatives by Mrs Mutch and Helen, who had been there in domestic service with my mother since she left school. Eric Simpson the joiner, who had been at school with me, came with his quiet efficiency and took charge of the arrangements (as he had done with my mother) though he himself, poor lad, did not have long to live. Dad's immortality had ended, as Mam said it would, and there was only a sheet to pull up and a dram to pour and a quiet prayer to offer in the stillness of the Buchan night.

Chapter Twenty-three

View from the Hill

Essentially I am a peasant, rising from the stock of the land, so it has been no surprise that I have wandered the world and felt an affinity with bedouins in the Sahara Desert and innocent tribes in the thickets of the Malayan jungle. A man can escape from the confines of his beginnings and take on layers of sophistication but he cannot escape from himself. When you peel away the veneer of our civilisation there are bonds which are as old as time itself and which tie us without yield to the places of our sunrise.

So I have come on this sentimental journey to look again on the soil which gave me roots and what better night to come than Hogmanay, a watershed in the Scottish psyche? Outby the night is crisp and clear, half-lit by a moon which casts its glow o'er parks and crofts and village houses down below, a world that hovers between reality and fantasy and makes a man stop to wonder where the known might end and the unknown begin. Here I am on Banks Hill, at the other side of the valley from Honeyneuk, with an elevated view of the village of Maud. Down there lies Fedderate Cottages, where I was born in the front room of a but-and-ben those many years ago, and just behind it no. 2 Park Crescent, which is filled with such happy memories. There is the path which led us to school and the playground where we jostled at cock-fighting or tackie or football and keeked over the wall as Doris or Mary or Margaret skipped and played rounders and squaries. Over there lies the Market Stance of the feein' markets and cattle floats and Dick's Circus; down to the right the station where I first watched the horses coming round from Aikey Fair and where we waved goodbye to the men who were off to war. Now a solitary engine hoots a plaintive call as a hundred years of bustling history comes sadly to an end. Down farther to the right the Low Village and the war memorial, where moss is gathering on those clear black names of yesteryear. Along to the hospital, or the Poorhouse as it was in those earlier days of the Dafties who slaved so hard.

On the grey horizon of a vanishing light, the Monument of Culsh points its fingers in the prayerful direction of heaven and beneath it now, ice-cold and still, lie the two who once found warmth and joy in my conception. Up here on Banks Hill those forty year ago we sledged on clear frosty nights like this and felt no need to contemplate a world that was heading for war and strife. This was our rural enclosure and we were safe and forever; and even when you flee the nest and come back again it seems as if you might never have been away. Was it all a dream? A fantasy? Did the Kremlin and the White House and the heights and the hovels and garish excitement of Hong Kong really exist? If so, they did nothing to break the thread of continuity which runs through the fabric of a people and will do so for as long as human beings will breed their own. Is it just my imagination or do I hear an organ playing quietly in the kirk below? Either way, I cannot but be stirred with love for my native soil as country voices soar into the heavens in plain sincerity. Perhaps it is in the singing of a simple hymn that people are drawn closest together, lifted out of themselves to a height of noble harmony which is beyond worldly explanation.

From the moonlit pool beneath comes the maudlin call of a Hogmanay drunk and a reminder that it is time to suspend the reverie and to stride down again to the maelstrom of living. The voices from the kirk come louder to meet me:

> A thousand ages in thy sight
> Are like an evening gone;
> Short is the watch that ends the night
> Before the rising sun

A GRAIN OF TRUTH

> Time, like an ever-rolling stream,
> Bears all its sons away;
> Then fly, forgotten, as a dream
> Dies at the opening day
>
> O God, our help in ages past
> Our hope for years to come;
> Be thou our Guard while troubles last
> And our eternal home.

By the iron railings of the kirk I pause to listen and to glance at the memorial in the corner. The spell is broken once more by a worldly wail of 'Nelly Dean' and the hooching and thumping in the village hall as mundane spirits cast themselves upon the helter-skelter of the eightsome reel. Yes, it is Hogmanay, an end and a beginning. A cursory glance around ensures that nobody is looking as I lunge my boyhood fervour at a well-shaped pebble which ricochets from kerb to dyke and back again, its echoes ringing eerily up the street and through the Bow Briggie.

Thus a Buchan loon embraces the scene of his childhood and finds a new warmth in the place where he began. Once more in the cradle, the wandering bairn drifts happily to sleep.